GREAT CLASSIC CARS

GREAT CLASSIC CARS

ALAN AUSTIN
CHRIS HARVEY

AN OUTSTANDING COLLECTION OF THE WORLD'S GREATEST MARQUES

CRESCENT BOOKS
NEW YORK

The authors and publisher would like to express their gratitude to Jim and Tony of the Art Company for the profile drawings and marque badges, to Delwyn Mallett for access to his Porsche and Mercedes, and to Barry Poulter.

DEDICATION

For two fathers, Arnold Harvey and Herbert Saunders who, together with XK Jaguars stimulated the author's and editor's interest in cars.

And for Chrystabel Austin, for her invaluable support to the artist.

This 1986 edition published in the
United States by Crescent Books,
Distributed by Crown Publishers, Inc
by arrangement with Octopus Books Limited.

Devised by Savitri Books Limited

© 1986 This edition Savitri Books Limited
© 1986 Illustrations Alan Austin

Printed in Hong Kong

ISBN 0-517-61671-8

CONTENTS

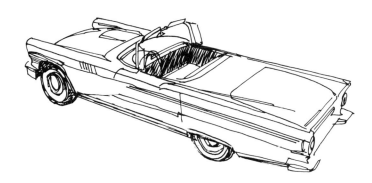

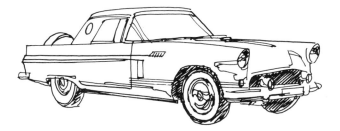

INTRODUCTION

Defining a classic car is simply a matter of deciding which model made by which of more than 5000 manufacturers in the past 100 years was so good that it was unforgettable. Unfortunately there have been so many models made by so many manufacturers that some have had to be left out to make such a list feasible to compile and digestible to read.

So the cars in this book have been selected not only because they were all classics, but because they were among the greatest. Again, with more than a million different cars from which to choose, some classics have had to be left out. The choice, therefore, tends to concentrate on the cars of which the author and illustrator have particularly fond memories. And because they are both still relatively young men, their selection includes a higher proportion of cars of the recent past than of those that have been long forgotten and bear little relation to anything normally seen today. It is inevitable that the 'nostalgia line' will move forward to exclude, say, the Clockenwerkenmobile of 1910 as more important cars emerge in later years. Age alone cannot be a qualification as to what makes a car one of the great classics.

Nevertheless, the Alfonso Hispano Suiza, first built in 1912, has to be high on any list. It was the first real sports car, and a joy to drive, in distinct contrast to many of the earlier high-performance machines from other manufacturers. Other fast cars, which were not 'beasts' of the road, tended to be neither as fleet as the Alfonso, nor as nimble. And none could illuminate the surrounding countryside like a lighthouse!

The Isotta Fraschini Tipo 8 that followed seven years later was by comparison very heavy to drive, but was such a magnificent machine that it has to be included. It is amusing to note in retrospect that the people who owned these extraordinary Italian cars were every bit as glamorous as their machines, so much so in fact, that they rarely drove them personally, and hardly spared a thought for the perspiring chauffeurs who had to wrestle with the steering. Some of the finest coachwork ever seen on a motor car and the world's first straight eight-cylinder engine were the most memorable aspects of the great Isotta.

The Austin Seven that first appeared in 1922 could not have been more different. It achieved the status of a national pet in Britain by displaying such virtues as extreme economy, reliability and charm. Deficiencies such as a 'sudden death' clutch and – by modern standards – an appalling lack of braking power together with remarkable quirks of handling were accepted as the norm by people who had never travelled in a car before. For many years there was nothing to touch an Austin Seven as an owner's first car.

At the other end of the price scale, the sports cars produced by Alfa Romeo for races such as the Mille Miglia and Targa Florio outshone all others in the late 1920s, not only because of their fabulous performance, but because they were so reliable. Of the numerous variants on this supercharged 1750cc theme, the Testa Fissa – or fixed cylinder head model – used by the world's greatest racing driver, Tazio Nuvolari, was the most memorable.

Alfa's greatest rivals in this sphere were Bugatti and Mercedes. The Bugatti Type 37A was, without question, one of the most beautiful cars ever made, as befitted the brainchild of a great artist, Ettore Bugatti. Not only were Bugattis beautifully styled and made, they handled so well that they invited comparison with thoroughbred racehorses. The Mercedes sports cars of this era were quite different, massive machines which were veritable juggernauts. But, like the Bugatti and Alfa, their highly-supercharged engines produced a great deal of power, with nothing more likely to chill the heart of a rival than the scream of the blower on the best Mercedes of all, the lightweight SSK.

In some circumstances, such as at the classic Le Mans 24-hour road race, Bentleys from Britain and the Stutz Black Hawk from the United States could run with, and beat, the Italian Alfas, the French Bugattis and the German Mercedes. No Bentley is more fondly remembered than the blown 4½-litre, although normally aspirated examples were far more successful. And no contemporary came closer to running these formidable Bentleys into the ground than the Black Hawk.

The Stutz's great rival in America was the fantastic 7-litre supercharged Duesenberg SJ that was capable of 161mph (260km/h) even though it was officially a touring car! But every manufacturer in those years had his price: the SJ's creator, Fred Duesenberg, fell prey to Errett Lobban Cord, possibly the greatest-ever car salesman. Cord was the most brilliantly persuasive talker of his time and the styling that he inspired approached the same standards. Little did it matter that his Auburn Speedster was in many ways a cheaper version of his Duesenberg, it was as great a classic because of its sensuous appearance. The cars that Cord produced under his own name were even more extraordinary, none better remembered than the coffin-nosed variants, although the 'Forgotten Cord', the L-29 was a more significant car.

As E. L. Cord's empire collapsed like a house of cards, General Motors forged ahead in America to become a corporation so unshakeable that it might have been made of solid rock. The brain behind this venture was one Alfred P. Sloan, who deserved the title of General for the way he rallied his forces to the principle that the corporation must cater for its customers from the cradle to the grave. Thus when they were young and strapped for cash, they could buy a cheap and reliable Chevrolet on hire purchase, then progress through the various marques – all made by General Motors – to a top-of-the-range Cadillac, of which in the 1930s the V12 was the most exciting.

In fact, it was such a good car that it rivalled Britain's Rolls-Royce, which bought up Bentley after the blown models had helped to destroy their maker in 1931. Bentley's 8-litre touring car could have become the best in the world, but Rolls-Royce maintained that reputation with its rival, the Phantom II. Packard was the only other manufacturer capable of competing with these two models with its V12, while other rival marques, like Mercedes, sold fewer exotic cars. Germany remained one of the most outstanding nations for craftsmanship, however. Truly amazing cars like the Horch 670 were intended to last forever!

For a while, Britain's flag in the sports car field was flown by Aston Martin, with the 1935 Ulster road-racing model as the greatest creation of a firm more interested in competitive glory than in profit. The first four-wheeled Morgan that appeared the following year became an absolute classic and its appearance remained essentially unchanged for the next 50 years. It still shows no signs of departing from the philosophy that a sports car should look like a sports car, no matter how modern the mechanical parts that power it.

Morgans have been able to survive almost as mobile anachronisms by limiting production to rather less than market demand. M.G.'s equivalent, the T-series that appeared at the same time, in 1936, endured for 19 years in one form or another and helped to establish the biggest sports car factory in the world at Abingdon in the centre of Britain.

In the same year, slightly further up-market, William Lyons, one of the best stylists in the world, built his first Jaguar sports car, the SS100. He then went on to establish a firm which has become one of the most profitable in the industry because it produces cars of such outstanding performance at relatively low prices.

Lagondas were in a totally different league, their magnificent V12 of 1937 being the creation of Walter Owen Bentley, who never made anything cheap; meanwhile Bugatti continued on his own sweet way with his most fabulous car, the Type 57SC Atlantic coupé, which must remain the definitive exotic. Its looks inspired Lyons when he produced a fixed-head coupé on is first sensational post-war sports car, the XK120, which appeared initially in 1948 in roadster form, with the world's first twin overhead camshaft hemispherical head production engine. Previously such exotic machinery could only be found in the likes of the Alfa Romeos raced by Enzo Ferrari, who eventually went his own way after the war with his first truly great sports car, the 212 barchetta, the appearance of which is still being copied today.

Rolls-Royce was eventually persuaded to produce a really sporting Bentley, the Continental, in 1952. It promptly became the world's fastest saloon car, and showed what the normally staid firm could do when it really let itself go. Cadillacs of this era were gargantuan machines, none flashier or more symbolic of America at the time than the Eldorado convertible – a proof that a hard-working breed of newly-rich youngsters had really made it.

Italy was still the home of true automotive sophistication. The Lancia Aurelia 2500GT became the world's first grand touring car, establishing new standards of handling and security of travel.

Mercedes remained defiantly traditional, concentrating on the engine above all for performance. But when allied with the spectacular coachwork found on the gullwing coupés of the mid-1950s, the package overcame inherent handicaps like swing-axle rear suspension to become a true classic. Contemporaries, such as Porsche, using a similar system, made cars which were even trickier to handle because the engine was in an extreme rearward position. But like Mercedes' customers, Porsche enthusiasts loved cars like the Speedster so much that the German firm eventually took over from M.G. as the world's leading sports car maker.

Ford, meanwhile, which had built a great reputation from producing stodgy cars – notably the world's most popular, the Model T – seemed to undergo a real revolution with the Thunderbird in 1957, as Facel Vega in France waved goodbye to a world of old-time opulence with the HK500

The heart of any car is its engine, and none demonstrated this more clearly than the little alloy gem which powered Buick's Skylark in 1960. No chassis was more significant than that of the world's most beautiful GT car, the Lotus Elite, which only really went into production in the same year. No body brought past glories more strongly to mind that that by Zagato on the Aston Martin DB4GT in 1961 and none seemed to presage the future more than Jaguar's E type – based on the 1950s D type sports racer – which helped to make it the first 150mph (241km/h) car that was within the means of most motorists. Ferrari's fantastic 250GTO only a year later stands as the last great front-engined sports racing car and Ford finally came good in the sporting stakes with the Mustang 289, which sold more than 60,000 in its first three days against Ferrari's total of just 40 in three years.

Chevrolet won the muscle car stakes, making the ground tremble with the power of its rumbling V8 engine in the Corvette Stingray which reached its zenith with disc brakes in 1966. At the opposite end of the scale, the British Motor Corporation had produced a worthy successor to the Austin Seven in the Mini, the world's smallest car which could carry four people in some comfort. Unlike the original Austin Seven, this product of a true genius, Alec Issigonis, handled in superb fashion, so safely, that it was possible to uprate its power to such a level that it had become a consistent world-beater in competition by 1966.

The Italian firm of Maserati hung on to a reputation established by the glories of past grand prix long enough to produce the stunningly attractive Mistrale grand touring car in 1967, the year that Ford swept all before it with the last great sports racer which could be driven on the road, the GT40. Cars are romantic vehicles, often produced by romantic people, and none more so than Alejandro de Tomaso, whose GT40 clone, the Mangusta, was distinguished by the inspired styling of Giorgetto Giugiaro.

BMW's 'Batmobile', the styling of which caused an unforeseen design revolution with spoilers, splitters and air dams all over the place, was a fantastic road-going competition car, whereas Ferrari's equivalent, the Daytona, was his last great front-engined GT, becoming by pure chance a successful competition car. Porsche's outstanding product of the same year, 1973, the Carrera RS, was never intended as anything other than a production competition car, but, ironically, became recognised as the firm's greatest ever road car.

Lamborghini's Countach remains the greatest modern day wonder, however, as the car with a unique shape that no-one else could successfully copy, and the one with performance unrivalled for more than a decade. No car has greater presence than a Lamborghini Countach, which makes it the greatest classic road car.

Badge and name reflect the nationality
of the car's manufacturers:
Damian Mateu (Spanish),
Mark Birkigt (Swiss)

1912 Alfonso was named in honour
of the then Spanish King — an
enthusiastic racegoer and expert driver

HISPANO-SUIZA ALFONSO

Beautiful Grebel headlight
from a 1923
Hispano Suiza H6B

IF YOU DEFINE a sports car as a road machine that is an absolute joy to drive, as nimble and fleet as any sprinter, yet blessed with the unflagging stamina of a mechanical marathon runner, then the Hispano-Suiza Alfonso was the first real sports car. All sporting vehicles before it were designed primarily for competition, and it was merely a happy coincidence if they could be used for a secondary purpose. That said, the Alfonso was spawned from a racing car, the Hispano-Suiza voiturette, which won the 1910 Coupe de l'Auto in France.

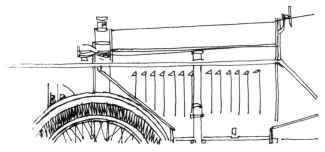

One of the early patrons of these cars from Barcelona was the teenage King Alfonso XIII of Spain, who was frequently to be seen dashing around the Catalonian countryside, clad in helmet and goggles, a military aide by his side. Good King Alfonso was an exceptionally fast driver and it has been said that the rigid posture adopted by his aides was probably reinforced by fear. For years his stable was never without one or two examples of what was to become the Spanish national car, the first pure sports machine being named after him in 1912.

It was at this time that Hispano-Suiza became known as a French marque too. A factory opened in Paris, to assemble the Alfonso and a range of heavy luxury carriages for the local market, and it started to develop its own lines. This was a natural progression because the French market was far richer than the Spanish, despite the continued patronage of King Alfonso.

The Alfonso was by far the most popular of the early cars, however, accounting for many of the 19,000 Hispano-Suiza vehicles built in Barcelona between 1904 and 1943. French production, on the other hand, totalled only 3000, concentrating on exotic machinery, often with V12 cylinder engines.

To the Spanish, Hispano-Suiza represented far more than a superb motor car. Their Swiss designer, Marc Birkigt – who gave the company its name in 1904 – was also responsible for a range of wonderful V8 cylinder aero engines, of which 50,000 were produced by 21 different companies, 90,000 20mm cannons and more than 100 million rounds of ammunition. It goes without saying that his cars were as well-engineered as his armaments; and that they were beautifully built. But what set them apart was Birkigt's artistry, matched only by that of the French-domiciled Italian, Ettore Bugatti.

Every part of a Hispano-Suiza, even the foot pedals, displayed an exquisite feeling for form. It was also incredibly well-balanced, the weight of the Alfonso being carried almost equally by each wheel. Furthermore, the weight was modest because everything was designed with such elegance. The swan's-neck spring hangers, for instance, looked delicate by the standards of the day, yet they were so well-stressed they never showed signs of strain.

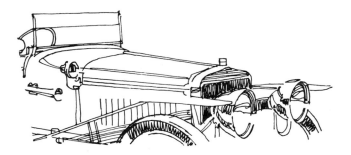

Because the Alfonso weighed a scant 2215lb (1005kg), when all around it were leviathans of double the bulk, Birkigt was able to employ a relatively rigid chassis of steel channel reinforced with hardwood. It did not need to flex like its heavily laden rivals. Therefore the Alfonso could use soft springs, giving a ride more like that of a modern car and an agility quite extraordinary among its peers. The T-head engine, only slightly detuned from that of the 1910 racer, was easy to handle because it had an exceptionally long stroke, endowing it with a great deal of pulling power. You could, if you wanted, drive a Hispano-Suiza in top gear all day, but you rarely did because the gearbox was such a delight to use. In those days, long before the arrival of synchromesh, considerable skill was needed to change ratios without grinding the gears like a miner extracting metal from rock. As befitted a manufacturer of magnificent guns, Hispano-Suiza showed they could machine cogwheels with such precision that they slid in and out of mesh without sound or vibration. The brakes were primitive, of course, but you could slow a Hispano-Suiza reasonably well on the gearbox alone.

You could also drive it at night faster than almost any other car on the road. This was because the Alfonso was equipped with extraordinary headlights. They were made of brass in three sections, the rear one hinged for access to the gas burner, vent and reflector. The centre section featured a finely honed Fresnal lens with a bull's-eye in the middle, protected by the front section carrying a flat outer lens. These fantastic lights were made by none other than Blériot, who built the first aircraft to fly the Channel to England from France. Small wonder that water held no fears for the intrepid pilot. His firm made lamps for French lighthouses. Heaven help anybody who met a Hispano head-on at night – it was like driving straight into the sun.

As the Alfonso philosophy was carried on by more mundane machines and commercial vehicles in Spain, the French Hispano-Suizas became ever more exotic. The H6B of 1919 was the last word in transport for the rich. Its six-cylinder 6.6-litre engine displayed the most advanced technology, developed in the air for the 1914-18 war. Its steel-lined cylinder block was made from aluminium with a single overhead camshaft and 7-bearing pressure-lubricated crankshaft. Like that of the Alfonso, this long-stroke engine produced a great deal of torque. And like the Alfonso, the H6B had a light, yet rigid, chassis. With so much power and torque, you could drive it from 8 to 86mph (13 to 138km/h) in top gear. But unlike the Alfonso, you could stop with ease, such was the efficiency of the servo-assisted brakes on all four wheels. It needed only a 110mph (177km/h) 8-litre short-chassis sports model, the Boulogne, in 1924 to bolster the marque's reputation.

Then, despite the Depression which gripped the Western world, Hispano-Suiza produced their biggest, most complex and most expensive design in 1930. This was the 9.25-litre V12 which took them through to the onset of the 1939-45 war.

After the war the factory in Paris never recovered, but the home base in Barcelona carried on producing Pegaso commercial vehicles and 125 Ferrari-like grand tourers bearing the same name. These were even more fabulous than Pegasus, the flying horse of mythology, but like the stork which was Hispano-Suiza's symbol, they were intended to show that the Spanish could make magnificent machines to rival the best in the world.

SPECIFICATION

Country of origin: Spain.

Manufacturer: Hispano-Suiza.

Model: Alfonso.

Year: 1912.

Engine: 4-cylinder in-line, side-valve, 3616cc.

Transmission: 3 forward ratios, live rear axle.

Body: Open or closed, 2 or 4 seats.

Wheelbase: 104in (2650mm) or 118in (3000mm).

Length: 161in (4100mm) short-wheelbase; 175in (4450mm) long-wheelbase.

Height: 57in (1450mm).

Width: 52in (1321mm) short wheelbase; 55in (1397mm) long-wheelbase.

Maximum speed: 70mph (112km/h).

The IF badge. The company was formed in 1900 by two young socialites, Cesare Isotta and Oreste Fraschini, they began building their own cars in 1904

The 6.6-litre Tipo 8 was designed by Giustino Cattaneo one of the most brilliant engineers in Italy. It was the world's first production car with a straight eight engine. Bodies were frequently so heavy that the big Isotta was capable of only around 70 mph (112 km/h). Illustrated is a 1922 sporting tourer

ISOTTA-FRASCHINI
TIPO 8

Isottas had some of the most splendid coachwork ever created for some of the most splendid customers

ISOTTA-FRASCHINI TIPO 8

ITALY'S GREATEST LUXURY car, the Isotta-Fraschini Tipo 8, will be remembered not so much for its splendid construction but for the glamour surrounding the people who were lucky enough to own a model. At one point the list included American 'nobility' like Rudolph Valentino, William Randolph Hearst, and Jack Dempsey; other aristocratic owners included a king (of Egypt), a queen (of Rumania), an empress (of Abyssinia), seventeen princes, four princesses, four maharajahs, a maharani, numerous dukes, duchesses, barons, counts and viscounts, the Aga Khan, Benito Mussolini . . . and the Pope.

It was not that Isotta lacked anything technically: the Tipo 8 was the first production car to be powered by that magnificent creation of the 1920s, the straight-eight engine, after the marque had pioneered brakes on all four wheels. But the price, four times that of any comparable luxury car short of a Rolls-Royce or Hispano-Suiza, every bit as much as its graceful bodywork by coachbuilders Sala, Castagna, Farina and Touring, guaranteed an exclusive clientele.

Isotta's ancestry was, of course, immaculate in the Italian tradition. It was a family firm started in Milan by lawyer Cesare Isotta and technicians Vincenzo, Antonio and Oreste Fraschini, with Cesare marrying the daughter of a wealthy family, Maria Bianchi Anderloni, Vincenzo wedding her sister Dolinda and Antonio completing the family circle by marrying a third sister, Carla. Oreste obstinately remained a bachelor while the sisters' brother, Felice Bianchi Anderloni, started the renowned Carrozzeria Touring to build bodies for Isotta-Fraschini chassis with another lawyer, Ponzoni, and Vittorio Ascari, brother of racing driver Antonio Ascari. Significant-

ly, however, all technical direction was left to an outsider, Giustino Cattaneo, who was to become renowned as one of the most brilliant engineers in Italy.

Cattaneo's early Isottas had a definite bias towards competition as a means of proving their reliability, and as such carried advanced features like overhead valves and camshaft. More than 50 different models were marketed between 1900 and the First World War in 1914, with especially strong sales in America. At one point, in 1906, Isotta-Fraschini was second only to Fiat as Italy's largest car producer. But by the time they pioneered four-wheel brakes in 1910, they were concentrating on costly high-performance machines which offered a higher profit margin on each car sold. Although Cattaneo's cars were primarily of sound and robust design, it was their engines which distinguished them. With few exceptions, they were very large and powerful, so it was hardly surprising that Isotta-Fraschini became one of Italy's main suppliers of aviation and marine engines during peacetime as well as war. They also built some formidable armoured cars.

Such was the success of their war effort that Isotta-Fraschini decided to concentrate on one model after the war – the big, heavy, and very profitable Tipo 8. This model remained in production with its 6-litre straight eight-cylinder engine from 1919 to 1924. Many of the lessons learned in the air were featured in the engine, notably the use of an aluminium crankcase and light alloy pistons. No less than three gallons of oil were pumped round the 10 main bearings at a time when many manufacturers were relying on splash-and-hope supplies. Cooling water from the vast front-mounted radiator was also fed to the cylinder block and head under pressure. A single shaft-driven unit combined magneto, generator and voltage regulator for an electrical system which was unusually refined for its day.

Such was the torque produced by this long-stroke engine that, despite two tons or more of solid steel chassis and bodywork, first gear was needed only when starting on a hill. Needless to say, the vacuum-boosted brakes were fantastic, with a mechanical linkage arranged to provide identical pressures on opposite wheels. The suspension reflected equal attention to detail, spring rates being meticulously matched to the weight of each complete car. Everything was so beautifully made that it was possible for the chauffeurs invariably hired to drive an Isotta to do so with great precision – adding to the magnificent aura that by now surrounded the marque.

Cattaneo still lusted for success in competition, however, and after the engine had been bored out to give 7.4 litres for the Tipo 8A of 1925, a sports model, the Tipo 8AS, was produced. Although still a bulky machine, the slightly lighter Tipo 8ASS (Super Spinto) won the Targa Abruzzo races in 1925 and 1926 for one wealthy customer, Duke Pio Arati di San Pietro. He then helped to start the famous Mille Miglia road race around Italy and the Tipo 8ASS maintained its reputation by taking sixth place in 1927 for Bindo Maserati, whose brother Alfieri had taken over as Isotta's chief test driver from Vincenzo Fraschini.

Production of all Tipo 8 models amounted to around 1350 with at least half of them exported to the United States. As a result, when Wall Street crashed, so did Isotta's car-making prospects as they resolutely stuck to very extravagant models. At one time it looked as though a merger with Ford might save them, but any such idea was killed by an Italian government dependent on Isotta's efforts with aero engines. Many of the government-sponsored Schneider Trophy racing aircraft had Isotta-Fraschini power, other units being made under licence as far away as the Soviet Union.

With no demand for such expensive luxury cars, only a few Tipo 8Cs were produced before Isotta-Fraschini was bought out in 1932 by Count Caproni di Taliedo to supply his aircraft business. Cattaneo resigned the following year and after that only aero engines and trucks were produced until Isotta-Fraschini prospered once more in World War II.

In a valiant, but vain effort to recreate the luxury car market, a new V8-engined Tipo 8C, called the Monterosa (after the street on which Isotta had lived), was produced as a prototype in 1947. But the world was not yet ready again for such a fabulously expensive concept and Isotta had to be content with producing engines for ships, trains, planes and anything other than very costly cars.

SPECIFICATION

Country of origin: Italy.

Manufacturer: Isotta-Fraschini.

Model: Tipo 8.

Year: 1919.

Engine: 8-cylinder in-line, overhead valve, 5898cc.

Transmission: 3 forward ratios, live rear axle.

Body: Open, 4 seats.

Wheelbase: 146in (3710mm).

Length: 185in (4690mm).

Height: 70in (1790mm).

Width: 69in (1750mm).

Maximum speed: 87mph (140km/h).

Despite its tiny size,
the 'Chummy' was a
full four seater
—just!

Conceived by Herbert Austin, the Seven
was a successful attempt both to solve
a financial crisis at the Austin works
and to produce a big car in miniature.
It sold prodigiously well and made
a fortune

AUSTIN SEVEN CHUMMY

Simplicity was the key to the Austin Seven's low price, with equipment confined to the bare necessities — note big lever for ignition advance and retard on steering boss

AUSTIN SEVEN CHUMMY

THE AUSTIN SEVEN was the car which stole the heart of the British nation. This was partly due to the fact that it was very cheap, was made in large numbers, and enabled many people to own and drive a car for the first time. It was also an amazingly long-lasting machine, which meant that even more first-time drivers learned to handle a car in an even cheaper second-hand Austin Seven. But whether they were new or old, Austin Sevens had some extraordinary quirks which made them easy to drive badly and difficult to drive well. Bad drivers were thrilled to be able to cope with the car and good drivers gained much satisfaction from overcoming basic deficiencies. Apart from the Model T Ford, produced in even greater quantities, the Austin Seven probably introduced more people to motoring than any other car. As it was, it decimated the market for motor cycles and sidecars by providing equally economical transport in more comfort.

Despite the Austin Motor company's penny-pinching attitude in the production of the Seven, it was a very tough and reliable motor car because it was made from good materials and by first-class workers. Cars like this established such a good reputation for the British motor industry that it became a dominant force in many export markets before going into decline with inferior products. Nations which copied the Austin Seven or produced it under licence included Japan with the emergent Nissan motor company, Germany with BMW, and the United States where Bantam produced the first Jeep.

There was little originality in the Austin Seven,

however. The first seven-horsepower Austin built in 1910 was a single-cylinder copy of the Swift, made in the same factory, and the Austin Seven which appeared in 1922 took its inspiration from Peugeot's Quadrilette. In between these two had come bigger Austins, making Herbert Austin one of the top manufacturers in Britain but leading him to the edge of bankruptcy. More than a quarter of a million people bought new Austin Sevens and helped to restore his fortunes.

The first Sevens had a 696cc engine before production got fully under way in 1923 with the definitive 747cc unit. This had a bore of only 56mm, which kept the taxable horsepower rating down to 7.8 for a licence costing £8 ($12) a year. This was a massive attraction in Britain where it then cost three times as much a year to tax the larger Model T Ford. Because of the narrow bore, the Austin Seven had to have a long stroke, 76.2mm in the 747cc unit which gave it a lot of torque or chugging ability. This also meant that the engine was understressed and lasted a long time, which was fortunate considering how cheaply it was made.

For years the engine had a tiny thin crankshaft with only two main bearings. It whipped in the middle and relied on sheer luck for lubrication. Once the engine was running, so much oil sprayed around inside that some droplets, inevitably, penetrated the bearings: there was no pump. The first models had an amazing device to give early warning of possible bearing trouble. It included a diaphragm made from the entrails of a pig, which had a tendency to rot, allowing hot oil to drip all over the passenger's knees. Such odd accidents were greeted with much amusement by drivers who were just thankful that the car kept going.

The chassis was as simple in its construction as the engine. It amounted to two steel girders braced in the middle like the capital letter A. Quarter-elliptic springs made up the bottom part with a half-elliptic spring slung across the top. Everything flexed to such a degree that the Austin Seven displayed the sinuosity of a mountain goat when clambering along the numerous unmade tracks of the day. This lack of rigidity also contributed to its incredible handling.

The spring across the front had little to anchor it against sideways movement. This meant that the car swayed from side to side as each wheel rode over a bump.

Most motorists who bought an Austin Seven knew no better and just accepted that the car had to be kept in rein, moving the steering wheel from side to side in a sawing motion in rhythm with the bumps. Fortunately, this was the best thing to do in any case. The effect was made more dramatic when the inside rear spring flattened as the body rolled while taking a corner, and the outside spring arched in sympathy. The rear axle then pivoted around its final drive and steered the car the opposite way to the front. But the driver, not knowing how a car should handle, corrected automatically. The back of the car then countermanded the steering, the driver corrected again, and it carried on back and forth until the bend had been negotiated. The ride was also very bouncy until the wheelbase was extended by six inches (153mm) in 1932.

Early models were called Chummies because their occupants had to be on very good terms with each other to squeeze into the tiny open body which had two seats at the front and a bench at the back for children, livestock or anything else which could be carried. Later models had a variety of bodies, to make the Seven into a saloon, van, truck and, with more power, a sports car. Ultimately, supercharged ver-

sions won major races and a series of brilliant twin overhead camshaft single-seaters was developed at great expense. But all Austin Sevens had a clutch pedal with about 0.25in (6mm) of travel. This 'sudden death' clutch proved highly amusing as Austin Sevens, no matter how ancient, leaped forward like kangaroos when driven by the uninitiated.

Braking could be equally perilous. The Austin Seven was one of the first cars to have brakes on all four wheels, but they did not work very well. This was because they represented the cheapest way possible to comply with the law decreeing that a car must have two independent braking systems. Thus the back ones were worked by foot and the front ones by hand with gloriously cheap and inefficient cables and levers. The brake drums at the back were too small to be worth much and the front axle twisted so much that the others – which were more important – lost even more power. But Herbert Austin maintained that good brakes led to bad driving and people who knew no better coped somehow. The Austin Seven became a classic because it changed people's way of life to such an extent that they wondered how they had ever coped without it.

It was also so small that numerous examples were kept in barns and outbuildings long after the model was replaced in 1939, while larger cars were broken up for scrap. The survivors became something of a national pet.

SPECIFICATION

Country of origin: Great Britain.

Manufacturer: Austin.

Model: Seven.

Year: 1925.

Engine: 4-cylinder in-line, side-valve, 747cc.

Transmission: 3 forward ratios, live rear axle.

Body: Open, 2 seats, shelf at back.

Wheelbase: 75in (1905mm).

Length: 109in (2768mm).

Height: 58in (1473mm) hood erect.

Width: 40in (1016mm).

Maximum speed: 52mph (84km/h).

The Type 37 was a sports car adaptation of the successful Type 35 grand prix car

Every detail of a Type 37 was pure sculpture—here is part of the front suspension

Engine was a straight eight, developed from the Type 30 by way of the Type 35 grand prix car

The Type 37's purity of line made it one of the most desirable Bugattis

BUGATTI

BUGATTI T37A

Bugatti design is all about beauty. Every car displays an elegance in engineering that must be attributed to the artistic genius of their creator, Ettore Bugatti. And they all performed exceptionally well for their day, some better than any of their peers. But in the continuing pursuit of superior performance, some of them had downright ugly bodies. So, no matter how well they performed, they cannot be regarded as the greatest Bugattis. Others were so big as to be clumsy. So they cannot be called the greatest even if they were the biggest. That honour must fall to the smaller cars, such as the Type 37A, which was an absolute gem.

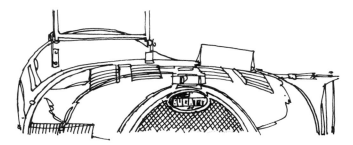

Ironically, it was also one of the cheapest Bugattis because its construction was relatively simple. But its purity of line transcended the more exotic specification of other Bugattis to make it one of the most desirable. Oddly, however, in a line of cars distinguished by the slogan *Le Pur Sang des Automobiles* – The Thoroughbred of Cars – the ancestry of the Type 37A was far from immaculate. It is equally ironic that Bugattis, adopted as the French national car, were the creation of an Italian designer.

Ettore Bugatti was born in Brescia, the son of a great furniture designer, Carlo Bugatti, and elder brother of the sculptor Rembrandt Bugatti. But it was Ettore's mechanical masterpieces that immortalised the family name. Some of his sayings were famous too. Bugatti has long been remembered for proclaiming in 1919, when castigated for building a very rapid racing car with very poor brakes: 'I build my cars to go, not to stop!' In the same vein, when the owner of one of his very expensive creations complained that, unlike an Alfa Romeo, it started only with considerable difficulty on a cold morning: 'If you can afford one of my cars, you can afford to

heat your motor-house!' And when questioned as to why the engine of another model was fitted with neither dipstick nor oil filler, Bugatti was alleged to have replied: 'My engines are assembled with the utmost precision and with their oil already in the sump. If you wish to replenish the oil you must return the car to my factory for the proper attention!'

With characteristic extravagance, he had a hotel bearing the name L'Hostellerie du Pur-Sang built next to the factory, which dominated the hamlet of Molsheim – pronounces Moles-hime, not Moll-sheem – in Alsace. The idea was not only to accommodate customers awaiting an audience with Bugatti in what was almost a feudal estate, but to emphasise the qualities of fine breeding, in machinery as well as horseflesh.

Bugatti had arrived in the Alsace area of eastern France from his native Lombardy to design cars for a variety of industrial concerns which then found themselves saddled with his imperious attitude towards customers who dared to complain. There was no doubt that Bugatti could design great cars but he lost job after job because he was intolerant of people who treated them like workhorses. It was only when the Spanish banker de Vizcaya – an enthusiastic amateur racing driver who owned a hunting lodge near Molsheim – helped to set Bugatti up in his own business at an old dye works that his greatest work saw the light of day.

The first car to bear Bugatti's name was the Type 13 – Le Patron refused to concede that earlier designs belonged to former paymasters – a little beauty called Brescia of which 435 were made between 1910 and 1920; one of them won the small car class in the 1911 French Grand Prix. From an early age when he rode a motorised racing tricycle for an Italian manufacturer, Bugatti understood only too well the advantages to prestige and publicity that success on the racetrack could bring. The very advanced 16-valve four-cylinder 1.5-litre racing Brescias stood him in good stead when the capacity limit for grand prix cars was reduced to 2 litres. Bugatti fitted their competition chassis with new eight-cylinder engines intended for a larger touring car, but as he failed to provide these Type 30 cars with adequate braking, their success was limited. The potential was obvious, however, and when the minor problem of stopping the Type 30 had been solved, Bugatti redesigned it to accommodate a ghastly 'streamlined' body, which was promptly christened The Tank. Again his design proved wanting, as the slab-like body caused the Type 32, as it was called, to almost lift off the ground. But in theory at least it was years ahead of its time . . .

It was only at this point that Bugatti began to look to the long-term future of his business, and decided to return to a slim and conventional exposed-wheel racing car like those of his rivals, Fiat and Sunbeam. While the Type 32 had been one of the ugliest cars ever made, its successor, the Type 35, was, without question, one of the most beautiful. Its dimensions were as dainty as those of the Brescia, and its execution even lovelier. The detail work was extraordinary. While Fiat pointed proudly to a rounded axle bored like a gun for light weight, in place of a conventional crude girder, Bugatti went one better and forged a hollow front axle into a more elegant shape with square holes machined to take the springs. He also provided the Type 35 with superb fully-compensated brakes on all four wheels.

Although Bugatti's earlier attempts in this area had featured the more advanced hydraulic operation – and failed through lack of development – the new layout reverted to cables, laid out with such perfection that they were a joy to use. Such was the beauty and nimble handling of the Type 35 that it became as big a success as the Type 32 had been a failure. All that was needed was for Bugatti to relent again and fit a supercharger in 1926 – Fiat had been using them since 1923 – for the Type 35 and its derivants, including the Type 39, to sweep all before them.

But these roller-bearing grand prix cars were very expensive to build and Bugatti realised that he would have to produce something cheaper to capitalise on their success for the sports-car field. The result was the Type 37 with a small plain-bearing engine from his Type 38 touring car, and wire wheels in place of the exotic alloy spokes of the Type 35. Other elements, such as the magneto and later the brakes, came from sturdier touring cars, but they were married with such harmony that the Type 37 became one of the best Bugattis, especially when fitted with a supercharger as the Type 37A in 1928 for small car, or voiturette, racing.

SPECIFICATION

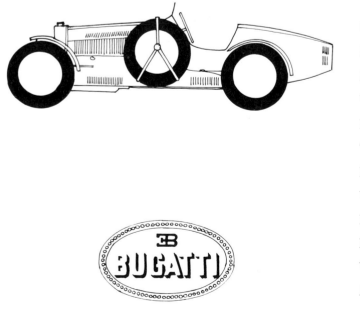

Country of origin: France.

Manufacturer: Bugatti.

Model: Type 37A.

Year: 1929.

Engine: 4-cylinder in-line, overhead camshaft, 1496cc.

Transmission: 4 forward ratios, live rear axle.

Body: Open, 2 seats.

Wheelbase: 95in (2400mm).

Length: 150in (3800mm).

Height: 48in (1220mm).

Width: 48in (1220mm).

Maximum speed: 105mph (169km/h).

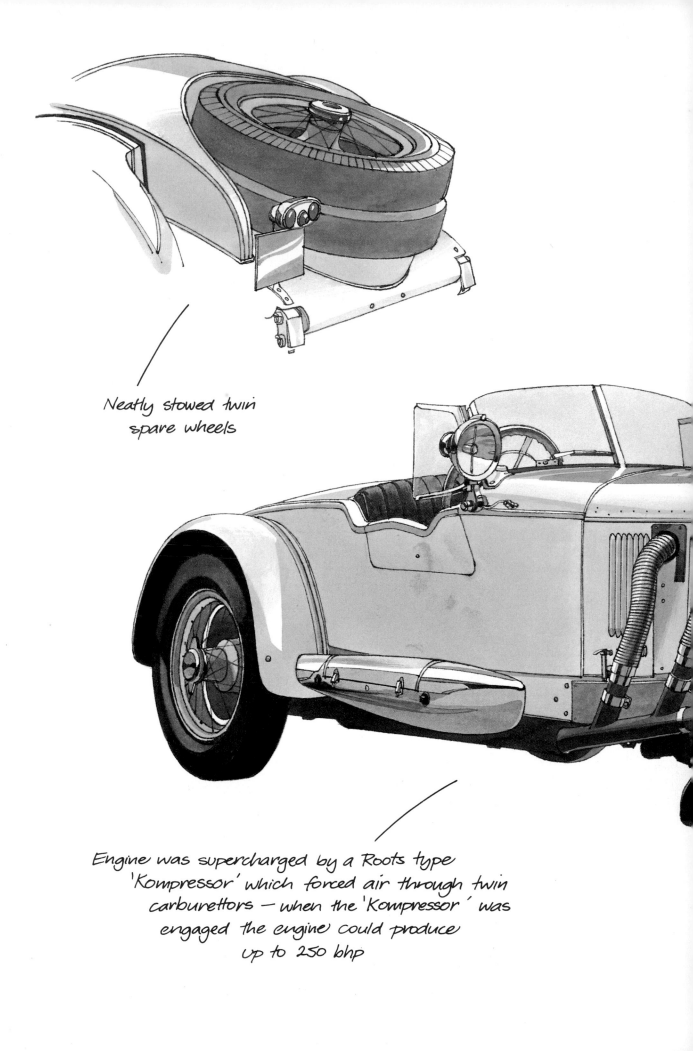

Neatly stowed twin
spare wheels

Engine was supercharged by a Roots type
'Kompressor' which forced air through twin
carburettors — when the 'Kompressor' was
engaged the engine could produce
up to 250 bhp

MERCEDES-BENZ SSK

SSK (K for German kurz = short) was originally designed
by Ferdinand Porsche and developed by Hans Niebel.
These lightweight models were among the
highest performance cars of their time
in the world

MERCEDES-BENZ SSK

THE MERCEDES-BENZ 27/170/225SSK – to give the Mercedes SSK its full designation – was one of the most awe-inspiring sports cars ever produced. Although it weighed at least 3750lb or 1½ tons (1700kg) it was capable of 125mph (200km/h) a speed at which its brakes were woefully inadequate on the open road. The fearsome spectacle of an SSK approaching at speed was heightened by the banshee wail from its supercharger, engaged through a special clutch as the throttle was opened wide for an extra burst of power.

The supercharging technology which gave the SSK its ferocious performance had been developed on Mercedes aero engines during the 1914-18 war as a means of dramatically increasing power without adding a great deal of weight. By the end of the war, the Daimler company which produced these engines knew as much as any firm about supercharging. As a result they were able to introduce two rapid new supercharged road cars in 1921: the 6/25/40 and the 10/40/65. The numbering system was quite logical once you knew how the Mercedes supercharging system worked. The first number represented the German taxable horsepower figure, the second the peak power before the supercharger was engaged and the third the maximum with the supercharger screaming away at full blast.

Both cars used a Roots twin-blade supercharger which pumped air under pressure into the engine's fuel-filled induction system. When mixed with fuel in the right quantity, more power could be produced than from a mixture sucked in under atmospheric pressure. This explosive mixture put the engine under more stress, particularly the cylinder head which formed the lid to the compression chambers. Mercedes engines were so strongly made they could stand a lot of extra pressure, but the compression

ratio still had to be kept fairly low. These massive machines also weighed more than two tons (2000kg) so they needed the extra power!

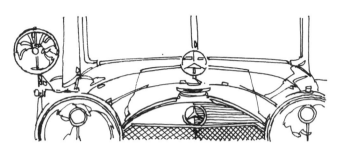

They were the last cars designed by Paul Daimler before, in 1922, he left the firm founded by his father and was succeeded by the legendary Dr Ferdinand Porsche, who had worked with Daimler's Austrian subsidiary. Porsche's first work for the parent company was to improve the supercharged cars, the last to be named, simply, Mercedes. His new 15/70/100 and 24/100/140 of 1924 used technology developed on an earlier supercharged racer. They became typical of the biggest and most expensive sporting cars of the 1920s, with a long wheelbase, chassis made from steel plates worthy of a steam engine, front axle girder seemingly taken straight from a railway bridge, live beam rear axle and very stiff springs. They stayed on the road chiefly because they weighed so much and the flexing chassis ironed out the worst bumps. All the same the ride was made tolerable only because of the length of their wheelbase and the depth of their upholstery.

The six-cylinder engines were similar to those of the earlier cars except that the supercharger at the front now became a 'blower' which forced air into the carburettor before fuel was added, rather than absorbing a certain amount of power by having to drive the heavier mixture from the carburettor into the engine. The new power units also featured an advanced and more efficient valve system operated by an overhead camshaft developed on Mercedes' last grand prix car in 1914. The mechanically operated brakes had not kept pace with engine development, however, and with massive top-heavy bodywork commensurate with their high price, these great vee-radiatored cars were formidable beasts to drive.

When Daimler and Benz merged to form what is now one of West Germany's biggest industrial combines, development of the supercharged machines continued as a new top line to the Mercedes-Benz range of cars, abbreviated to Mercedes, to the dismay of Daimler-Benz. Profits were high on each car built, but it was not possible to produce many because of the amount of work that went into them. Few people could afford them in any case.

One of the main problems with the 24/100/140 was handling, which was a challenge to any driver. Reducing the overall weight to make the car more agile became even more important than extracting more power from the engine. The easiest way to make the car lighter was to cut out a section of the massive chassis and attendant coachwork – so a short-wheelbase model called the K for *kurz* (or short) was introduced in 1926 for the more adventurous owner.

The brakes were also improved a little and a low-line version with an even more powerful engine, called the 26/120/180S, offered the short-wheelbase chassis at the same time for customers who did not mind climbing straight into their car rather than stepping up into their carriage. This lighter S-for-sporting model was much better to drive than the 26/100/140K or its more savage 26/110/160K variant because it had a new chassis with side rails swept high over the rear axle, lowering the centre of gravity along with the body.

In the unending quest for extra power, the engine was bored out to 7.1 litres for the 27/140/200SS (or Super Sports) of 1928. More dramatic developments included redesigning the cylinder head – the part of an engine where all the power comes from – to work with dual ignition and a higher 6.2:1 compression ratio in the 27/170/225SS later that year. It needed only further shortening of the wheelbase to produce the greatest supercharged Mercedes, the SSK, with either the more sedate touring engine or the searing high-compression engine.

In its more powerful form, the SSK (or Super Sports Short) was also a formidable car on the racetrack when driven by the brilliant Rudolph Caracciola. In three years from 1928, he won the German Grand Prix at the Nürburgring, the Tourist Trophy in Britain and the Mille Miglia in Italy. By this time the SSK had been developed further, with power increased at the expense of reliability in the 27/180/250SSK of 1929 and the ultimate 27/240/300SSKL (for Super Sports Short Light) of 1930. The maximum power of these higher-compression cars could be used only for short periods, however, before they blew the top off the engine. The engines also had to be rebuilt or replaced after every race they managed to finish.

Such problems rendered them impractical for normal use and left the SSK standing alone as the King of the Road.

SPECIFICATION

Country of origin: West Germany.

Manufacturer: Daimler-Benz.

Model: Mercedes-Benz 27/170/225SSK.

Year: 1928.

Engine: 6-cylinder in-line, overhead camshaft, 7065cc supercharged.

Transmission: 4 forward ratios, live rear axle.

Body: Open, 2 seats.

Wheelbase: 116in (2950mm).

Length: 183in (4636mm).

Height: 66in (1676mm).

Width: 68in (1727mm).

Maximum speed: 125mph (201km/h).

Stutz mascot was the Egyptian
Sun God Ra, the asp on the
forehead symbolising power

Only 55 Stutz Black Hawk DV32's
were built — the 32 stood for the number
of valves in the engine — a deliberate
publicity attempt to match rival cars
boasting V12 and V16 engines!

STUTZ BLACK HAWK
SPEEDSTER

DV32 straight eight engine had
twin overhead camshafts and
four valves per cylinder. The
322 cu.in. engine developed 156 bhp

STUTZ BLACK HAWK SPEEDSTER

WITHOUT A DOUBT, Stutz made the greatest sports cars America has ever seen. The first models were designed and built by Harry C. Stutz, an Ohio farm boy of Dutch descent renowned for his ability to 'fix anything'. This original shade-tree mechanic with little formal education had a dogged determination to do everything right, including building his own motor car.

As a result, his very first car, built largely from other people's components, rolled straight out of his garage in 1911 and finished 11th at the local track – Indianapolis! Its Wisconsin four-cylinder T-head engine had been highly successful in racing boats although it was not as refined as the power units in the rival Mercer or Marmon. But like the rest of the car, it was rugged and dependable. Stutz also kept an iron grip on his drivers, insisting they use only standard cars and drive for a finish rather than risk retiring in a mad burst of glory with a fragile highly tuned car.

Stutz cars gained an enviable reputation for re-liability, winning race after race while lesser machines fell by the wayside. Bearcat and Bulldog were two of the model names used during this early period for pure sports cars which could hold their own in any contest. When one customer returned his car complaining that the new single overhead cam 16-valve engine in his Bearcat was no good, Stutz gave the car to a daredevil motor-cyclist called Cannonball Baker, who – with little or no experience of four-wheeled motoring – promptly ploughed along primitive American roads from San Diego to New York in a sensational 11 days 7 hours and 15 minutes. Every conceivable record was broken with a shock absorber clip as the only casualty on this formidable reject of a car!

The factory, which had already been doing well on its racing successes, was swamped with orders and Stutz decided to refinance the operation so that he could step up production from 500 cars a year to 3500. Floating his business stock on Wall Street proved to be the undoing of Harry C. Stutz. It was promptly bought up by a financier, Alan A. Ryan, who forced up the price from $70 (£46) a share to $724 (£480) by methods which provoked a national

scandal and resulted in suspension of the stock on the New York stock exchange. Stutz was forced to quit in 1920 and went off to build the largely unsuccessful H.C.S. car before dying of appendicitis in 1930. The firm which bore his name was bought up by Bethlehem Steel millionaire Charles M. Schwab and bankers who knew nothing about making motor cars. They stopped the Stutz racing programme and sales plummeted as a result. It then became clear even to these financial men that a new model was vital.

It was also obvious to others and the men who approached the company with propositions included the engineers James Scripps Booth and Frederic Ewan Moskovics, who, entirely independently, had come up with highly refined versions of the American Underslung car designed by Harry Stutz in 1905! The erudite Hungarian-born Moskovics presented the better option and was given backing to hire a team of engineers, a brilliant team as it turned out, to develop his 'Vertical 8 with Safety Chassis' – to distinguish it from Packard's straight 8.

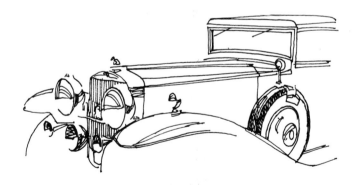

This new Stutz was a worthy successor to the outdated pre-1914 war machinery they were still trying to sell in 1925. The engine had an overhead camshaft, dual ignition, nine main bearings and forced-feed lubrication. As if that were not enough, it had a chassis to match with an underslung worm-drive rear axle, hydraulic brakes and side members several inches lower than any of the opposition. The running boards were designed to act as side bumpers and the glass was of pioneering safety design in that it had fine wires cast into it in a horizontal pattern aimed at minimising the effects of breakage.

This radical new car not only caused a sensation, but sold very well when it was found that its performance matched its looks, with excellent roadholding as a result of its low centre of gravity. Speed and acceleration were good, although speedometers which read ten per cent fast were fitted to create the illusion that they were the fastest cars on the road. As sales soared again, so did power outputs which culminated in the Black Hawk Speedster of 1927. One of these cars lapped the Indianapolis Speedway at 71.36mph (115km/h) without missing a beat for 24 hours. Stutz were back in the big time!

Speed king Frank Lockhart then contacted the factory for a chassis to use as the basis for a streamlined car to take the World Land Speed Record. Experiments with aerodynamics perfected a boat-tailed body which took the Speedster to a 96mph (154.5km/h) win in the Atlantic City 150-mile (240km) race. Lockhart then added a supercharger and far more radical aircraft-inspired bodywork. With personal backing from Moskovics, he survived one bad crash on Daytona beach before risking everything in difficult conditions for another try. He set a class D record for the mile which stood at 198.29mph (319.15km/h) for 32 years. Sadly, the record was a posthumous one, since he lost his life in the attempt. It was a bitter blow to Stutz and Moskovics, but not as bitter as the one they had suffered a week earlier.

In his efforts to publicise the Black Hawk Speedster, Moskovics had wagered $25,000 – £5000 at that time – with European bodybuilder Charles Weymann that the 5-litre Stutz could outrun any road car from across the Atlantic. Weymann chose a Hispano-Suiza because it had an 8-litre engine. Moskovics rubbed his hands in glee, realising that such a car was no match for a Black Hawk on its home ground at Indianapolis. It was an odd contest in that the high-revving Stutz with its superb handling and excellent brakes was far more like the European idea of a sporting car than the Hispano, which was very American in concept, with a large slow-revving engine for better low-speed acceleration, and a ponderous chassis. In the event, the Stutz's driver was so surprised at the way the Hispano took off that he over-revved his engine on the first lap of what was supposed to have been a 24-hour contest! The Stutz retired 750 miles (1200km) later . . . and a replacement promptly trounced the Hispano in a re-run.

The damage which had been done to the Stutz's reputation was not repaired even when Weymann – one of the few men who knew how close the Hispano had come to defeat – bought a Black Hawk, which came within an ace of defeating the previously all-conquering Bentleys at Le Mans. But then not many Americans had heard of Le Mans . . . and as few people could afford a Stutz after the Great Depression, the marque finally succumbed in 1935.

SPECIFICATION

Country of origin: United States of America.

Manufacturer: Stutz.

Model: Black Hawk Speedster.

Year: 1928.

Engine: 8-cylinder in-line, overhead camshaft, 4950cc.

Transmission: 3 forward ratios, live rear axle.

Body: Open, 2 seats.

Wheelbase: 131in (3327mm).

Length: 184in (4674mm).

Height: 54in (1372mm).

Width: 67in (1702mm).

Maximum speed: 105mph (169km/h).

Beautiful Gran Sport body is
an early example of Zagato design

Elegant tail
accommodates
twin spare wheels

Designed by Vittorio Jano.
The 1750 engine featured
twin overhead camshafts,
crossflow head and
supercharging. It developed
85 bhp at 4500 rpm

ALFA ROMEO 6C 1750GS

This car, with a top speed of 90 mph (145 km/h), is similar to the one in which Campan and Ramponi won the Mille Miglia in 1929

Note beautifully cast finned inlet manifold

ALFA ROMEO 6C 1750GS

THE GREATEST SPORTS cars during the classic period of the late 1920s and 1930s were produced by Bugatti and Alfa Romeo. That is not to say that the products of Aston Martin, Bentley, Jaguar, Mercedes and Stutz were not great, but none of them had that exquisite precision and delicacy of control which made a Bugatti or an Alfa Romeo unique. When the discussion turns to which is the greater, Bugatti or Alfa Romeo, the Italian machine has one considerable advantage: it is a far more practical everyday car, its French rival needing all the nurturing of a hot-house plant. And when the debate is carried to which was the greatest Alfa Romeo made during these years, there is only one answer: the 6C 1750.

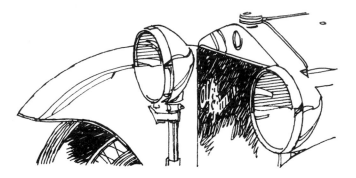

There were five principal variants in this range, all based on the same traditional chassis, with classical half-elliptic leaf springs front and rear and mechanical brakes on all four wheels. It may seem odd today, but they were also fitted with right-hand steering as standard. This feature is normally found only on cars intended for use in Britain, Japan and Australia, where it gives the driver better visibility from the car's normal position on the left-hand side of the road, the rest of the world driving on the right with the driver sitting nearest the centre of the road, on the left of the car. The reason the 1750cc Alfa Romeos were built this way was because they were sports cars first and foremost and races are, by tradition, run on clockwise circuits. This gives the driver of a car with right-hand steering the advantage of better visibility for judging the line through a critical bend.

Of the five varieties of 1750 Alfa introduced in January 1929, the short-wheelbase Super Sport and Gran Sport were the most exciting because they were

the lightest and fastest. In general, when these chassis were fitted with elegant and expensive bodywork by Farina, Simonetti, Touring or Zagato, they adopted the designation Gran Sport, the 'inferior' title of Super Sport being reserved for the cheaper and less exotic factory-built bodies, which typically had cycle-type wings. Of the more expensive bodies, the spartan beauty of the Zagato coachwork is much admired because it is the lightest and endows a 6C 1750 Gran Sport Alfa Romeo with the highest performance.

There was a further significant sub-division even in a production run that amounted to only 370 cars in three years: both Gran Sport and Super Sport Alfa Romeos could be bought with an optional supercharger, gear-driven from the crankshaft for maximum efficiency and fed with fuel under pressure through an exquisite finned inlet manifold. Not even Bugatti's casting could match this Milanese metalwork.

The final variant among these outstanding cars was the Testa Fissa, or fixed-head, Gran Sport competition model, of which only 12 were built. In this form the cylinder block of the very advanced twin overhead camshaft engine was cast in conjunction with the hemispherical cylinder head. It proved a very effective, if expensive, way of strengthening the engine to withstand a higher boost from the supercharger. The bottom end of the Testa Fissa engine was also strengthened to withstand the increase in power by fitting a crankshaft with eight main bearings instead of five, a work of art as marvellous as the manifolding. The potent Roots superchargers were lubricated by adding oil to the fuel, and when a vegetable-based substance, such as the popular Cas-

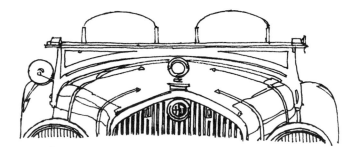

trol R (for racing) was used, they emitted a gloriously nostalgic smell that reeked of the racetrack.

These cars with their incredibly searing exhaust note won almost every important road race in 1929 and 1930, with outstanding performances in the arduous, round-Italy Mille Miglia, which swept all round Italy, and the Targa Florio, which took place on the tortuous mountain roads of Sicily. And the men who drove them became legends: Giuseppe Campari and Giulio Ramponi winning the Mille Miglia in 1929 and Tazio Nuvolari – acclaimed by many as the greatest racing driver of all time – beating his arch-rival, Achille Varzi, the following year. When both drove Gran Sport Alfas, starting only a minute apart on what was a 1000-mile (1600-km) time trial, Nuvolari knew there was only one way he could be sure of winning. He waited until nightfall, then drove like a demon through the twisting mountain passes, his lights extinguished in case his rival realised he was drawing ever closer. Nuvolari relied on lightning reflexes to avoid plunging off the rough mountain roads into deep ravines, safe in the knowledge that Varzi's hearing was drowned by an exhaust note every bit as deafening as his own. And then, once he was on Varzi's tail, there was no holding Nuvolari.

Varzi avenged his defeat in the Mille Miglia when he persuaded Alfa Romeo's illustrious designer, Vittorio Jano, to produce a special version of the P2 Alfa Romeo grand prix car on which the Gran Sport was based. The fearless Varzi reasoned that the sheer power of this savage machine would compensate adequately for the nimble handling of the Bugattis, which had dominated the only event the 1750 had – at that point – failed to win: the Targa Florio.

Predictably, this ultimate Alfa Romeo road car with a grand prix engine burned fuel at a tremendous rate, made worse by a leak in its massive tail tank. But those were the days of riding mechanics, and Canavesi was as fearless as Varzi. Twisting back in his seat, he plunged a funnel into the fuel tank's filler and poured in petrol as the ferocious Alfa Romeo bucked, swerved and howled through the countless bends of the race. Inevitably, fumes from the filler were ignited by the hot exhaust, but Canavesi braved the heat to snap the filler shut. With flames billowing from burning bodywork, Varzi and Canavesi scorched home to win the Targa Florio and put an end to French domination of the greatest event in Sicily.

It should be remembered that Alfa Romeo were able to produce such fabulous and expensive machines during the days of the Depression because they represented only a tiny part of the company's output of touring cars, agricultural vehicles and aero engines, built in conjunction with the Meridionali concern. It was, however, the supercharged Tipo 6C 1750 Gran Sport Zagato that brought romance to the name Alfa Romeo.

SPECIFICATION

Country of origin: Italy.

Manufacturer: Alfa Romeo.

Model: 6C 1750 Gran Sport.

Year: 1929.

Engine: 6-cylinder in-line, twin overhead camshaft, 1752cc supercharged.

Transmission: 4 forward ratios, live rear axle.

Body: Open, 2 seats.

Wheelbase: 109in (2745mm).

Length: 154in (3911mm).

Height: 48in (1219mm).

Width: 54in (1379mm).

Maximum speed: 110mph (177km/h).

Cord-developed 4934 cc straight 8 engine, producing 115 bhp at 3300 rpm, mounted with the clutch forward, the crankshaft turned counter-clockwise

Front wheel drive model, rare for any car of this period

1931 standard production cabriolet body made by LaGrande (Union City Body Company)

The Cord needed a big steering wheel to cope with so much weight over the front wheel

CORD L-29

THE L-29 HAS been called the Forgotten Cord because it stands in the shadow of the later coffin-nosed models which brought fame to their creator, Errett Lobban Cord. He was an outstanding sales-man, perhaps one of America's greatest, and a financial genius. Cord went bankrupt three times before bouncing back to make fortunes away from the motor industry in real estate, an early pop music radio station and finally, uranium.

His life could have been very different: he nearly struck gold with his first motor car. It was called the L-29 because it made its debut in 1929 with power from Lycoming, the aero engine wing of the Auburn car manufacturing company which Cord happened to own. He had acquired the decaying Auburn company of Indiana, and the legendary Duesenberg high-performance car makers, as part of a financial package put together for backers after he had been successfully running an agency for luxury cars made by the American firm, Moon.

Cord knew little about cars other than how to sell them. His engineering ideals were inspired far more by fashion than by practical considerations. From Auburn's base in Indiana, it was easy to see that front-wheel drive had a future as Miller racing cars toppled conventional rear-wheel drive Duesenbergs at Indianapolis. Cord knew that he could sell the advanced new front-wheel drive concept to the American public if it could only be contained in a car which looked *different*. Dispensing with the conventional propeller shaft between the transmission and rear axle would allow the seats to be mounted lower and the car to be made to look more rakish and aggressive. Cord sold himself on the idea immediately and bought up Miller's patents, and the Miller transmission engineer, Cornelius van Ranst.

Van Ranst pointed out that although the new transmission worked well on a racing car it would not necessarily do so on the road. As it stood, a tight turning circle was almost impossible to achieve. Cord replied that as it stood, van Ranst was the engineer and it was up to him to fix such problems: he needed front-wheel drive and a low-line body to sell the cars. Costs would be saved, wherever possible, by using components made by Cord's companies to allow more money to be spent on glamorising the car.

Cord was far from enamoured of the efforts of his resident stylist, Al Leamy, so he summoned project engineer John Oswald to follow him round the golf course. Between holes, Cord explained that he wanted a racy-looking car with tablespoon fenders (or wings), a chassis which would make it the lowest on the road, and a body along the lines of a Hibbard & Darrin show car displayed at the recent New York salon. Duly briefed, Oswald was dispatched back to town to draw up his plans on a blackboard in the Auburn car plant. His round of golf completed, Cord dropped into the factory, took one look at the chalk drawing, approved it, and appointed Oswald designer, draftsman, metal worker, body builder, engineer and foreman on the experimental L-29.

In the meantime van Ranst had devised a way of turning the straight eight-cylinder Lycoming engine round in the chassis to drive the front wheels through Miller's front suspension with new constant-velocity joints which reduced the turning circle from a mammoth 42ft (12,800mm) to a very tight 21ft (6400mm). All you need to solve engineering problems is a kick in the pants, said Cord. Oswald worked like a slave for two months to build the first prototype, incorporating a Leamy-designed radiator shell which disguised a driveline that was 6in (152mm) higher than normal. The Auburn town theatre was then cleared so that this L-29 saloon could be shown to the assembled plant personnel. They approved of the car which was to bring work to

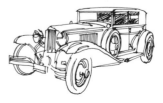

the Auburn plant, so it was sent to the company's test track – a ploughed field across the road – while Oswald and Leamy busied themselves designing a drop-head version. The test track was so bumpy that the saloon's doors flew open. Cord realised that they would have to stiffen the thing up, and instructed Auburn's chief engineer, Herb Snow, to sort it out. In desperation, Snow had two channel sections of steel welded across the chassis rails to invent the X-frame bracing which was to become a hallmark of American cars for the next 25 years. There you are, I knew you could do it, said Cord.

When the next prototype was rushed through, it was commandeered by Cord, who set out hell-for-leather on a 2000-mile (3200-km) trip to old haunts in Phoenix, Nevada (where he was later to become a State senator and discover uranium). Nothing fell off the car and Cord promptly leapt on a plane for New York, where he turned up to the astonishment of Auburn executives who were attending that year's automobile show. As a mechanic roared back to Auburn with the L-29, Cord burst in on the gathering to send terrified underlings scurrying about publicising the L-29. 'Years have been devoted to developing a car which needs no selling to those who can afford it,' said Cord, glossing over the fact that it had been conceived, built and tested in only eight months.

The motoring Press were wildly excited by this newcomer to a class dominated by stolidly conventional Packards, Chryslers and Cadillacs, all of which had taken years to hone to well-oiled perfection. The Cord's glamorous body and front-wheel drive more than compensated for the mundane mechanical components which had been lifted from Auburn and Lycoming parts bins. Top coachbuilders were excited by the opportunity to mount long, low, rakish bodies on to a chassis only 16in (406mm) from the ground at a time when the average was half as high again. None of them cared that the about-face engine concentrated its weight far back from the driven wheels, which thus lacked traction on a slippery hill. They were dazzled by the powerful appeal of a bonnet half the length of the complete car.

Unfortunately for Cord and the town of Auburn, Indiana, the public were not taken in, chiefly because the L-29 was priced at upwards of $3000 (£2000). People with that kind of money wanted a car which was perfect in every way. Even slashing $800 (£533) off the price failed to stir sufficient sales in a market hard hit by the collapse of Wall Street two months after the L-29's launch. After prophesying demand for at least 10,000 a year, Cord had to be content with 4500 over three years, before gambling again with even more adventurous coffin-nosed styling. The later cars proved even more costly fiascos, leaving the L-29 as a lingering memory of what might have been, had there been a little more time to achieve perfection.

SPECIFICATION

Country of origin: United States of America.

Manufacturer: Cord.

Model: L-29.

Year: 1929.

Engine: 8-cylinder in-line, side-valve, 4934cc.

Transmission: 3 forward ratios, live front axle.

Body: Open or closed, 2 or 4 seats.

Wheelbase: 137in (3480mm).

Length: 197in (5003mm).

Height: 75in (1905mm).

Width: 66in (1676mm).

Maximum speed: 77mph (124km/h).

This two-seater body was fitted
to the 4½-litre after the 1939/45
War but follows the lines
of earlier cars

Heavy duty heat shields
for outside exhaust

BLOWER BENTLEY

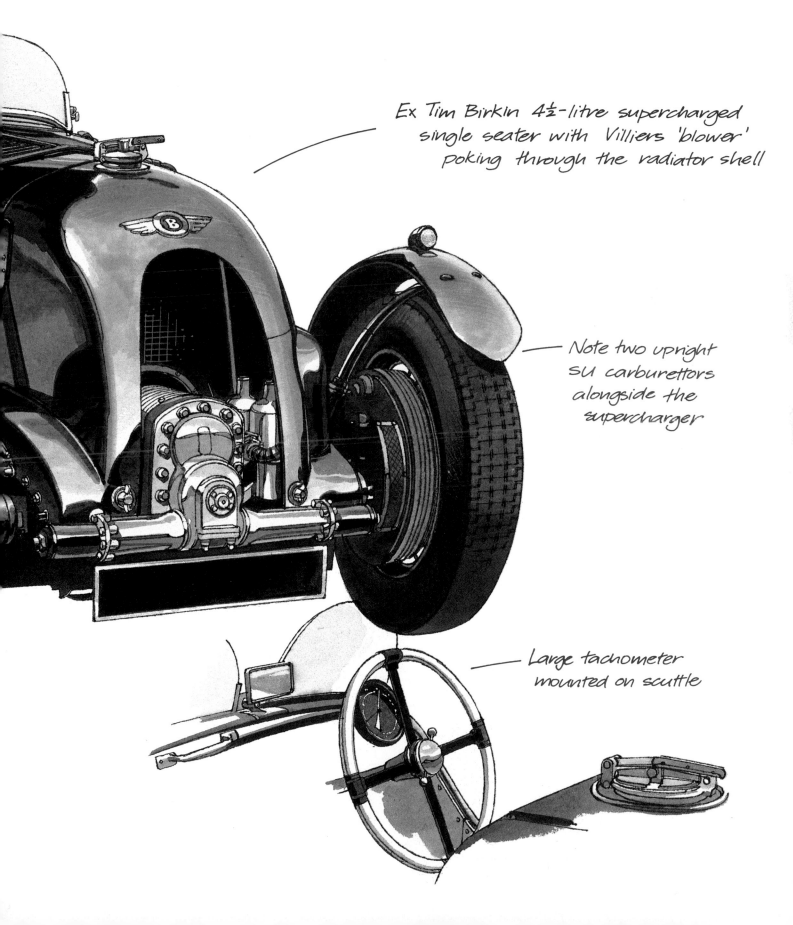

Ex Tim Birkin 4½-litre supercharged single seater with Villiers 'blower' poking through the radiator shell

Note two upright SU carburettors alongside the supercharger

Large tachometer mounted on scuttle

It is strange but true that the Blower Bentley which was, in its day, every boy's dream racer, and a symbol of the magnificence of British engineering, was shunned by its designer. To Walter Owen Bentley – invariably known as W.O. – engines were everything, and, as a former locomotive engineer, he rated reliability above all other qualities. If a car needed more power he would enlarge its engine, so that it was not over-stressed by adventurous tuning. But Bentley paid a heavy price for his love of massive powerplants. The chassis and tyres of his cars suffered from having to carry heavy machinery at high speeds over the rough roads of the 1920s.

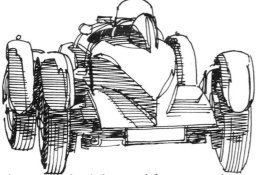

He also recognised the need for success in competition to boost sales against those of the 45 other British firms which had started making cars in the euphoria that followed the First World War. But he did not agree with his star driver, Sir Henry 'Tim' Birkin, that a lighter, more highly tuned engine was necessary to keep ahead of the opposition without imposing impossible demands on the chassis and tyres. When Bentley gave in and built his most famous car, the supercharged 4½-litre, it cost him his company.

The story started in 1914 when war broke out and Bentley found himself designing aero engines, of which the BR1 and BR2 rotaries were extraordinarily good. Bentley's role in Britain's war effort was also significant in that he persuaded most other aero-engine makers to use his advanced new aluminium alloy pistons. At the end of the war in 1918 a payment of £8000 ($12,000) enabled him to establish Bentley Motors in a small factory at Cricklewood, North London. As was only to be expected, the engine of the first Bentley was a magnificent affair. Although it had only four cylinders, it was very efficient, featuring an overhead camshaft operating four inclined valves per cylinder with a five-bearing crankshaft and, naturally, aluminium pistons. The rest of this first 3-litre car was of conventional high quality with a separate four-speed gearbox and sturdy chassis. Orders flowed in for the superbly built, and very expensive, car after a prototype won its first race at Brooklands in 1921.

These 3-litre Bentleys were notable not only for their speed, but also for their stamina. They excelled in a new branch of the sport – 24-hour racing over a closed circuit made up of normal roads – by taking fourth place in the first such event at Le Mans, France, in 1923. With more experience of such races and brakes on all four wheels, a 3-litre Bentley outdrove 40 other cars from France – then leading the world in racing car design – to win the race in 1924 and inspired Ettore Bugatti to say that 'Monsieur Bentley builds the fastest lorries in the world!'

Three litres was fine for a sports car, but Bentley realised that more power was needed to haul the heavy formal coachwork which many customers built on to his chassis. In essence, he added two cylinders to his 3-litre engine to produce an experimental 4½-litre Bentley in 1925. But when a prototype 7.7-litre Rolls-Royce proved just as fast, Bentley bored his six-cylinder engine out to 6½ litres to maintain his lead. This engine was also made to run far more silently, like that of a Rolls-Royce, by means of a very expensive triple connecting rod camshaft drive in place of the rumbling 4½-litre's vertical shaft. The pioneering use of rubber mountings for the engine contributed further to its advanced qualities.

But the cost of development was enormous and Bentley Motors found themselves in financial difficulties until 1926 when they received backing from racing driver Woolf Barnato of the Kimberley diamond mining family.

Freed, temporarily, from money worries, W. O. Bentley was able to design a new four-cylinder 4½-litre engine, using technology from both the 3-litre and 6½-litre, to produce 110bhp and a monumental amount of torque for Le Mans in 1927. The story of how the new 4½-litre and two supporting 3-litre Bentleys collided with two French cars at White House corner is well-known and so is that of the heroic drive by Sammy Davies and Harley Street consultant Dr. J. Dudley Benjafield to win with a surviving 3-litre.

Soon after 4½-litre cars started reaching customers, who were delighted with their retention of the 3-litre's four-cylinder 'thump' that was such anathema to the 6½-litre owners. Their sporting appeal was heightened when two of the Bentley team took first and fifth places at Le Mans in 1928. But Barnato, driving the winner with Bernard Rubin, could see trouble ahead when the frame of his car, hardpressed by an American Stutz, cracked under the strain four laps from the end. He realised more power was needed, but doubted whether a racing car could be built that was strong enough to take the 180bhp 6½-litre engine that Bentley suggested, without being impossibly heavy. Nevertheless, the Speed Six which resulted crushed all opposition at Le Mans in 1929 and 1930, after a struggle with an SS Mercedes.

Between races, however, Bentley's fortunes slumped as economic depression swept the world. And works driver Birkin doubted whether the Speed Six would win again at Le Mans in 1930 for much the same reasons as Barnato in 1929. But Birkin was possessed of great charm and managed to raise finance from the wealthy Miss Dorothy Paget to produce a series of supercharged 4½-litre Bentleys that had as much power as the Speed Six, but less weight. The only trouble was that Le Mans was for production cars and a run of 50 was needed to be eligible to compete in 1930.

At first W. O. Bentley would have nothing to do with the project, saying later that 'to supercharge a Bentley engine was to pervert its design and corrupt its performance', and he appeared to be right: Birkin's engines kept blowing up. But Birkin managed to persuade Barnato that they needed only a little more development and that it was worth producing 50 cars with the added magical attraction of a supercharger.

In the event, when the Blower Bentleys were running, they were very fast, beating all but one Bugatti in the 1930 French Grand Prix. But they retired with broken engines in races such as Le Mans and cost Bentley their reputation for reliability. The production run of 50 proved crippling, Bentley Motors went into receivership, and were bought up by Rolls-Royce in 1931 to race no more.

SPECIFICATION

Country of origin: Great Britain.

Manufacturer: Bentley.

Model: 4.5-litre supercharged.

Year: 1930.

Engine: 4-cylinder in-line, overhead camshaft, 4398cc supercharged.

Transmission: 4 forward ratios, live rear axle.

Body: Open, 2 seats.

Wheelbase: 132in (3353mm).

Length: 173in (4381mm).

Height: 66in (1676mm).

Width: 69in (1740mm).

Maximum speed: 125mph (201km/h).

This car was one
of the Harley Earl designs
bought in from California
by General Motors to
re-establish the Cadillac
image

Elegant tail concealed a 'dickey' seat

CADILLAC 370

V12 engine of 341 cu.in. was developed
from the far more glamorous 452 cu.in.
16-cylinder engine — but proved
far more practical
in operation

CADILLAC 370

THE CADILLAC 370 with its mere 12 cylinders, although probably the better car, has always lived in the shadow of the more glamorous 452 cu inch 16-cylinder model on which it was based. Sales certainly bore out this contention, with the V12-cylinder 370 eventually outselling the 452 by nearly 20 to one. And this was despite the fact that both cars were launched as the great American Depression was gathering momentum in 1930! Of course, General Motors did not intend to introduce them at a time of such economic blight. To understand the philosophy behind them, you have to understand the thinking of Alfred P. Sloan, who took over their manufacturer, General Motors, in 1923.

Sloan was convinced that the only way to survive by selling motor cars was to provide models which would accommodate everybody's needs – from the cradle to the grave. Thus, car ownership could progress from a starting point with his cheap Chevrolet, through Pontiac, Oldsmobile, Buick and La Salle to the top of the line: Cadillac – all the while keeping faith with the General Motors brand name. The theory was that Junior could be born at any time during this progression of ownership and still be indoctrinated to the General creed. Hopefully, General Motors would be able to provide the car of his dreams no matter what the state of his pocket. If the first car he drove as soon as he could reach the pedals was a Chevrolet, then he could be expected to aspire to owning a Cadillac one day. In Sloan's eyes, this made their expensive limited production models every bit as important as the volume-selling Chevrolets.

He was horrified, therefore, when in the 1920s Cadillac lost its leadership in the large car class to Packard, even though the shortfall in sales hardly made a dent in General's overall profits. Packard had established their lead by following the great European cars with V12-cylinder engines. This meant that Cadillac had to go one better to put Packard firmly in its place. The new Cadillac had to be faster, more powerful, more refined and have more cylinders than anything else on the road. It was no good simply enlarging the existing V8 to outrun the Packard.

Besides failing to forge ahead on prestige by having more cylinders, there were technical problems in building a transmission to cope with the extra torque which a larger V8 could be expected to produce. While it was worth investing in a new engine that was overtly superior to any other, it was not worth spending money on cogs that nobody cared about until they went wrong. In any case, General had plans for a new transmission system. The company was working with one Earl A. Thompson to adapt his Synchro-Mesh mechanism to take the clunk out of their corporate gearboxes and establish a marketing lead while their rivals ground their teeth in despair.

There were doubts at the time as to whether a Synchro-Mesh gearbox could be made strong enough to take the torque of a bigger stump-pulling Cadillac V8, so whatever new engine replaced it would have to have more power rather than torque. General's array of slide rules backed the V12 formation but their findings were promptly overruled by Sloan, who said that such an engine would forever be compared with that of the Packard, which had the advantage of having produced a V12 as early as 1915. Go to war on another four cylinders, commanded Sloan.

At that point General struck it lucky in that an exceptionally gifted engineer called Owen M. Nacker was appointed to develop the 341 series V8 – which made its appearance in the '27 La Salle – and then

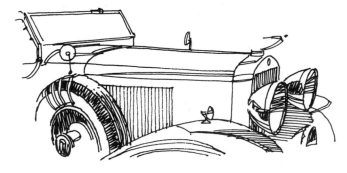

move on to Cadillac's V16. The entire project was cloaked in such secrecy that most of General's underlings thought that they were developing a commercial vehicle because everything needed for the new engine was marked Bus or Coach. Not only did Nacker's new engine run smoothly, as was only to be expected of one with so many cylinders, but the smoothness and silence of operation were almost uncanny. This was largely attributable to the use of an early form of hydraulic tappet, the first such use in a production engine. The gearbox and rear axle ran in harmony to emphasise the new car's qualities, which put it on a par with the British Rolls-Royce which was also being produced in America at the time.

In fact, a Rolls-Royce engineer, Maurice Olley, who had been working at the company's American plant in Springfield, was hired by General Motors to ensure that the new Cadillac's suspension was comparable. Olley ultimately developed independent front suspension for Cadillac in 1934 . . . but by then the V16 was doomed.

Sales were quite good in its first year, 1930, despite the Depression. Nevertheless, 350 of the 2850 produced remained unsold at the end of the year when new buyers were traditionally looking forward to a revised model. It was decided, therefore, to introduce a back-up model to counter possible criticism that 16 cylinders were too extravagant for these hard times and to avoid alienating potential future customers. This new Cadillac, the 370, used the chassis of the biggest V8 with a V12-cylinder version of the V16 that was every bit as smooth and silent as the larger engine. The chassis was relatively new in any case, having been introduced in 1928, so it rode practically as well as that of the V16 and was more manoeuvrable because it was lighter.

From that point on, at the end of 1930, the V12 and V16 enjoyed different sales patterns. As orders for V16s plunged, demand for the V12 rose with the rival V12s from Packard and Lincoln falling behind. Only 750 V16s were sold in 1931, despite heavy discounting by dealers which brought its price down to almost that of a V12! It seemed as though the Great American Public would not buy it at any price.

In 1932, sales of new V16s were down to 346 while the 370 stood firm on 1709. Cadillac, and Sloan, could hardly believe it and announced that they would build just 400 V16s in 1933 – one for each of the legendary Top Four Hundred of American society. In the event, the pocketbooks of most of the Top Four Hundred stayed closed: only 125 V16s could be sold, as against nearly 1000 V12s. And so the saga went on, with the V12 occupying the top spot on steady annual sales of around 900, as the V16 went down to 50, its rivals selling only by the handful. It proved once and for all to General that peasants were, if anything, more important than presidents.

SPECIFICATION

Country of origin: United States of America.

Manufacturer: General Motors.

Model: Cadillac 370.

Year: 1930.

Engine: V12 cylinder, overhead valve, 6019cc.

Transmission: 3 forward ratios, live rear axle.

Body: Open or closed, 2, 5 or 7 seats.

Wheelbase: 140in (3556mm).

Length: 190in (4826mm).

Height: 66in (1676mm) to 78in (1981mm).

Width: 68in (1727mm).

Maximum speed: Average 95mph (153km/h) according to body.

1929 Phantom II with chauffeur-driven coupé
bodywork by Kellner of Paris

Famous Rolls-Royce badge.
Soon after Henry Royce's death
in 1933 a change of colour
to black for the initials RR
was seen as a sign of mourning
for the great engineer

ROLLS-ROYCE PHANTOM II

Phantom II had a maximum speed of around 80mph
(128km/h) and did only 15 miles to the gallon (5.3km/litre)
but carried its occupants in the greatest luxury

ROLLS-ROYCE PHANTOM II

FOR MORE THAN half a century Rolls-Royce was the only contender to the title of 'Best Car in the World' – awarded by a journalist – and the qualities of latter-day aspirants are often open to question by comparison. It is equally difficult to decide which was the best Rolls-Royce produced during the marque's halcyon years.

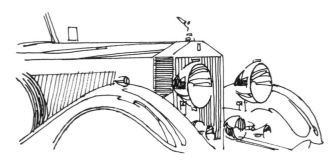

At first glance there might seem to be only one deserving model: the legendary Silver Ghost. But if truth be known, the Ghost's spectre could be tarnished by the demands of modern traffic. And the phenomenon which followed, the Phantom I, has been regarded, quite rightly, as only an interim model – a re-engined Ghost – on the way to Henry Royce's last great car, the Phantom II. This was not only the logical conclusion to his Ghostly theme, but a very much faster car that is still capable of keeping pace with modern traffic. In its most extreme configuration, the final Phantom II, the short-wheelbase Continental, was capable of 95mph (153km/h), displaying acceleration, handling and braking better than the majority of cars built 40 years later.

Henry Royce, master mechanic, did not claim to be a great innovator. He was concerned only with producing a motor car which was, to his eye, as near perfect as possible: a strong and trouble-free machine, smooth and silent, and good enough to last a lifetime. He was more proud of the fact that the Silver Ghost would accelerate smoothly from 3mph (5km/h) to 59mph (95km/h) in top gear than the fact that it helped to pioneer the six-cylinder engine. The governor gear used on the Ghost, and still retained for the Phantom II, was an excellent example of Royce's concern for the owners of his cars. It was coupled to the accelerator linkage in such a way that it kept the engine running at any set speed, regardless of load, up to half-throttle. Thus Rolls-Royce chauffeurs who had attended a special course organised by the works could change gear smoothly and silently without any special sensitivity of ear, hand or foot. In fact they could do so in extreme old age just as well as when they had all their youthful faculties.

The value of this device was especially evident in the early days of motoring when many chauffeurs were of mature age, and set in the ways of driving a coach and horse. The mechanical governor which overcame the most formidable obstacle to driving a car worked like this: it could be set at a particular point in its sector so that when the speedometer indicated a certain speed, the clutch could be withdrawn and a smooth gear change effected because everything that revolved was in perfect harmony.

Such a device, like every other fitting on a Rolls-Royce, was only perfected as a result of a series of drawings and modifications which was not finalised until Royce was satisfied that it could be improved no further. The process was even more lengthy when, owing to ill-health, caused by years of overwork, Royce spent long periods living far from the company's works in Derby, either in the South of France or on the south coast of England. Wherever he was, he was always attended by a permanent staff, to translate his ideas into a seemingly never-ending stream of drawings. These were relayed back to the factory for development, eliciting reports requiring further action from Royce and which resulted in yet more drawings. Royce's motto was 'rub out, alter, improve, refine,' until – with the eye of an artist as exacting as Ettore Bugatti – the final polished product met with his approval.

He also devised a bumping machine which could subject his chassis to the rigours of thousands of miles of rugged roads in only a few hours. As a result, Rolls-Royce were justifiably proud of an unparalleled reputation for reliability, any hint of a mechanical problem being dealt with immediately by the factory at no expense to the owner. This philosophy has been retained to a large extent today and certainly prevailed when Ghosts and Phantoms were current. Such a reputation for reliability also made Rolls-Royce ideal candidates for defence work involving new-fangled aero engines, a line which they were to pursue as a separate entity from automobile engineering.

Although the Silver Ghost stayed in production from 1906 until 1925, early models varied a great deal from later ones as a result of Royce's constant pursuit of perfection. He would not be rushed into anything. Royce resisted suggestions that the Silver Ghost might benefit from brakes on all four wheels until 1924 when he had perfected his mechanical servo, which then stayed in production for 30 years.

The new engine, which distinguished the Phantom I chassis (Rolls-Royce did not at that time build their own bodywork), had a longer stroke for even greater flexibility, so that it could carry heavier formal bodywork without any loss of performance. It also had a detachable cylinder head for easier maintenance, like the smaller 20hp Rolls which had been introduced. But a radiator with vertical shutters rather than the horizontal ones fitted to the smaller car made recognition easy.

While other makers of luxury cars suffered during the Depression, Rolls-Royce thrived, due in no small part to the success of their aero-engine business. It was during this period, from 1929, that the Phantom II came to represent the zenith of Henry Royce's achievement, and as such the most perfect motor car he had ever designed and built. Earlier criticisms of high-speed harshness in the Phantom I engine were countered by fitting a heavier crankshaft which restored every element of the Ghost's silky smoothness. An automatic lubrication system was fitted to the chassis that eventually became almost one-shot, in utter contrast to the 99 points which needed weekly attention on the earlier cars.

Henry Royce was fulfilled by the Phantom II and the aero engines which won the Schneider Trophy races in 1929 and 1931. He worked right up to his death in 1933, and soon afterwards the initials RR on the Phantom's radiator were enamelled in black instead of red. It was immediately seen as a sign of mourning for one of Britain's greatest engineers. But, in reality, the directors who kept Rolls-Royce running as smoothly as ever had agreed on the change before the death of Royce . . . because black, unlike red, never clashed with an owner's colour scheme. Black could stand alone, like a Phantom II.

SPECIFICATION

Country of origin: Great Britain.

Manufacturer: Rolls-Royce.

Model: Phantom II Continental.

Year: 1931.

Engine: 6-cylinder in-line, overhead valve, 7668cc.

Transmission: 4 forward ratios, live rear axle.

Body: Open or closed, 2, 4, 5 or 7 seats.

Wheelbase: 144in (3658mm) or 150in (3810mm).

Length: 200in (5080mm) or 206in (5232mm).

Height: 66in (1676mm) to 78in (1981mm).

Width: 66in (1676mm).

Maximum speed: Average 90mph (145km/h).

SSJ belonging to Clark Gable with body by LaGrande; one of only two short-chassis cars produced; purchased by Gable in the fall of 1935, the other was owned by Gary Cooper

Supercharged engine reputed to deliver 400 bhp and 140 mph (225 km/h)

Exhaust pipes had a silencer by-pass offering 'full-throated' motoring

DUESENBERG SJ

Instrumentation was more than adequate and included such items as altimeter, barometer, stopwatch chronometer, brake pressure gauge and an oil-change warning light

DUESENBERG SJ

IF EVER THERE was a car built to satisfy the tastes of Hollywood it was the Duesenberg SJ, a phenomenal creation weighing upwards of two and a half tons (2500kg) which had a supercharged 7-litre twin overhead camshaft straight eight-cylinder engine that propelled it at more than 70mph (113km/h) in first gear, 100mph (160km/h) in second and 140mph (225km/h) in top. Mildly tuned versions were capable of 161mph (260km/h), an almost unheard-of speed 40 years ago. A typical cross-section of people who bought such cars was even more illuminating, consisting as it did of diplomats and gangsters, debutantes and political bosses, robber barons and religious leaders, all incredibly rich and very discerning. It took a Duesenberg to match their income bracket.

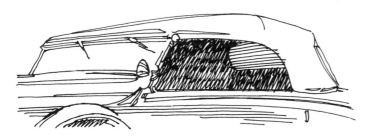

Film star Gary Cooper, for instance, spent the money he made from a starring role in *Lives of a Bengal Lancer* on a short-chassis SSJ in 1935. But what did it matter? He was about to become a superstar with *Mr Deeds Goes to Town*. No sooner had he had the one and only SSJ bodied by Errett Lobban Cord's LaGrande coachbuilding concern, than his arch-rival Clark Gable wanted one too. So Augie Duesenberg built another, costing Gable a great part of his income from the blockbuster *Mutiny on the Bounty*.

Most of the longer Duesenberg SJs had four seats and carried three people: a chauffeur in the front and the owner, and his, or her, chosen companion in the back. Only one disciple of Duesenberg, a maharaja, is reputed to have had enough rupees to buy the ultimate, a long-wheelbase two-seater with boat-tail body by Murphy of New York.

Four hundred and eighty of these Duesenbergs were built in either supercharged SJ or normally aspirated J specification. Even the ordinary Model J was good for 250bhp at a time when a 770K Grosser Mercedes struggled along on 200. The J just made the New York Auto Salon in December 1928 as a result of superhuman efforts by the German-born, American-reared and self-trained engineering genius Frederick S. Duesenberg, and his brother, August S. Their achievements over 40 years had taken in every form of transport from bicycles to tractors, aero engines to racing cars. Then they were bought out by Cord who inspired them to even greater efforts. He saw the Model J as a loss leader to promote interest in a cheaper range of cars. The fabulous Duesenberg engine, lifted almost unaltered from racing cars good enough to win at the local Indianapolis track, was built by Lycoming to improve the status of the old straight-eights which powered Cord's bargain-basement Auburns.

Despite their price, and the demand for such an exclusive car, Duesenberg never made money. They cost so much to make that even in their best years the total raised from sales only just covered the materials, with no allowances for overheads. The eight-cylinder engine was all of 4ft (1220mm) long and finished in apple-green enamel with masses of nickel, chrome and stainless-steel fittings. That's what the customers saw. But inside, it was even more exotic with four valves per cylinder. And then there was the chassis frame made from the best chrome steel, fully 8½in (216mm) deep and nearly one quarter of an inch (5.5mm) thick. Even the instrument glasses were bevelled from the finest crystal.

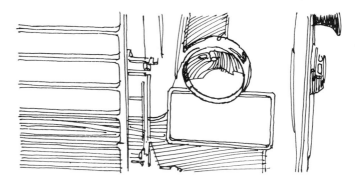

The panel they were mounted in was made from machine-turned aluminium to save weight, as were the pistons, connecting rods, bell housing, sump, timing chain and camshaft covers, water jackets and pump, intake manifold, brake shoes, drum surrounds, final drive casings and numerous smaller fittings. If there was a way of turning a component from solid metal forging, Duesenberg would do so rather than risk cutting the cost with a casting which might crumble in the next century. Their cars were intended to be timeless and even today show every likelihood of lasting for ever. The sensation this rolling chassis created when it was first seen at the New York Salon was enough to send Auburn's sales soaring.

It also sent coachbuilders' pulses racing. The finest in the land, Judkins and Willoughby, Derham, Rollston, Brunn, Weymann, Bohman & Schwartz, Brewster, Woods, Kirchoff and Walton, jostled for the privilege of building a $3500 (£2333) body on an $8500 (£5666) Duesenberg chassis for customers who could afford skyscraper-sized bills. And even then they didn't make money because every car was a one-off with seemingly endless exclusive features to outshine a rival's products. Building a Duesenberg body was the nearest an American coachbuilder could get to displaying a Royal warrant.

European equivalents such as Barker and Gurney Nutting in Britain, D'Iteren and Vanden Plas in Belgium, Hibberd & Darrin, Fernandez, Kellner, Franay, Figoni & Falaschi, Letourneur et Marchand, Saoutchik and Cattaneo of Paris in France, Graber in Switzerland and Castagna in Italy, did it for money, creating some of their most memorable bodywork on this great chassis at prices approaching $25,000 (£16,500). These were subsequently emulated by the errant Mr Cord's Union City Body Company, suitably renamed LaGrande for the occasion.

If Frederick S. Duesenberg considered the Model J his baby, the SJ was his magnum opus. When supercharged, the engine – which Augie had been tuning up to 285bhp for selected customers – unleashed 320bhp at a mere 4750rpm and proved capable of propelling these formidable machines from rest to 100mph (160km/h) in just 17 seconds. And yet these massive machines, although truck-like to manhandle at parking speeds, displayed a quite unexpected delicacy of handling for their bulk once in motion. In marked contrast to the average American leviathan of later years, they also stopped very well, such was the size of their finned and power-assisted brakes.

Thankfully Duesenberg lived long enough to see his SJ completed, although a crash in a Murphy-bodied convertible hastened the end of a restless life, racked with pain from arthritis and, later, cancer. It is easy to speculate on what he might have achieved had he survived longer than his 55 years. But at least he died happy in the knowledge that the SJ had been acclaimed as 'The Finest Car in the World'.

SPECIFICATION

Country of origin: United States of America.

Manufacturer: Duesenberg.

Model: SJ.

Year: 1932.

Engine: 8-cylinder in-line, twin overhead camshaft, 6882cc supercharged.

Transmission: 3 forward ratios.

Body: Open, 4 seats.

Wheelbase: 142in (3607mm).

Length: 200in (5080mm).

Height: 66in (1676mm).

Width: 68in (1727mm).

Maximum speed: 140mph (225km/h).

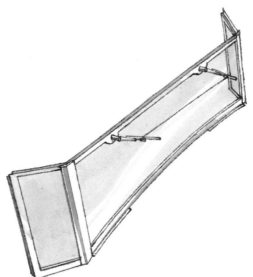

Note the unusual 3-piece windscreen—
later copied by Hupmobile and Panhard

The Horch V12 was quite literally
designed to last forever!

Formed in 1932 the Auto-Union combine of Horch, Audi
DKW and Wanderer produced this splendid V12
Spohn-bodied cabriolet

HORCH 670

THE HORCH V12 was not only a magnificent motor car produced in the most adverse circumstances but one which could trace its ancestry to the dawn of the motor industry. Indeed, it was redolent of an age when young craftsmen were sent wandering through Central Europe to learn their trade as journeymen. No matter that Horch's greatest car was designed by Fritz Fiedler who later achieved fame at BMW with high-performance cars and aero engines. It was conceived as a last defiant gesture to demonstrate that there would always be a market for the products of engineers as skilled as Karl Benz, Gottlieb and Paul Daimler, Wilhelm Maybach and August Horch. All had a hand in the Horch V12 whether they knew it or not.

Karl Benz has been called the father of the motor car because in 1885 he produced the first motorised carriage for use on the road – a tricycle – with four-wheeled cars to follow soon after. At about the same time, only 60 miles (96km) away in another part of southern Germany, another superb engineer, Gottlieb Daimler, was starting the company which would make Benz's greatest rival. Daimler and Benz never met, but their machines were among the most advanced produced anywhere.

One admirer, Emile Jellinek, became a Daimler director and named the cars he sold after his daughter Mercedes. Soon all German Daimlers, designed by the founder's assistant, Wilhelm Maybach, were called Mercedes, while the products of allied companies in Austria and Britain continued to be called Daimler. Benz were their greatest rivals but kept pace only in fits and starts of indecision. Wilhelm Maybach left in 1907 to set up his own company producing gargantuan cars and aero engines, and Gottlieb's son, Paul, returned from Austria to take over as chief engineer.

Meanwhile another young journeyman, blacksmith's son August Horch, had wandered as far as Budapest to learn his craft on the railways before he saw his first car at the age of 27. He wrote to the maker, Karl Benz, to ask for a job and was soon made plant manager in charge of 70 employees. But he left two years later in 1898 when Karl Benz was squeezed out of his own firm, accused of being too conservative

in the face of the threat to sales from Maybach's advanced new Mercedes.

Horch managed to borrow enough money to start making his own cars in 1899, rapidly acquiring a reputation for employing advanced new technology. But he tended to put quality before profit and spent the rest of his life constantly trying to raise enough money to develop new lines. In 1910, like Benz before him, he found himself forced out of the firm he had founded. But he hit back and started building cars called Audi, the Latin equivalent of his German name, meaning Listen! or Hark!

The cars now built by August Horch then performed better than the cars still being built under his name; but he made the mistake of concentrating on big expensive cars after the 1914-18 war. In the economic depression which followed, sales slumped to such an extent that he found himself in 1920 on the road again, wandering like a journeyman while the Horch and Audi factories carried on making cars without him.

Horch were in such severe trouble that they were taken over by the Argus aero-engine makers. Amazingly, they promptly hired Paul Daimler, a chief engineer in the same mould as Horch, who had fallen out with his father's old firm! He was responsible for a magnificent succession of Horch cars, featuring straight 8-cylinder engines like those of Isotta-Fraschini, but more advanced with single and, later, twin overhead camshafts.

While August Horch travelled throughout Germany, reporting on new advances in technology for the Transport Ministry, Audi floundered and, in 1928, were taken over by the Dane Jørgen Rasmussen, who built small but successful DKW cars of advanced design. Recession gripped Germany the following year and Paul Daimler was among those made redundant when DKW and Audi joined Horch and another firm from Saxony, Wanderer, to form

Auto Union, in a joint fight for economic survival. With a fine display of nostalgia, August Horch was reinstated as a director and he returned to the splendid halls of Horchwerke for the first time in 20 years. But his influence was minimal as another former journeyman, the Austrian Dr Ferdinand Porsche, was hired to design their great state-subsidised racing cars.

Meanwhile Fiedler, who had replaced Paul Daimler at Horch, was responsible for the magnificent V12, aimed not so much at Mercedes as Maybach, who had been making the only 12-cylinder German car. The theory was that because ordinary people could not afford a new car during the Great Depression, it was only worth making very profitable ones for the lucky few who could finance such extravagances. Maybach, and Voisin, in France, creamed the profits from such extraordinary vehicles because their main business was in aero engines, which absorbed the development costs. Horch failed because there were not enough car buyers who could afford to pay for their dreams.

Nevertheless, the Horch type 670 was an incredible machine. It was a tribute to Teutonic concern for craftsmanship and was intended, quite literally, to last for ever. Its huge water-cooled side-valve engine was designed for durability and enormous pulling power rather than high performance, with a drive train engineered to such fine tolerances that it worked in a silent way which was wonderful for its day. In company with the engine it was mounted on hydraulic dampers to insulate the occupants of the car from any noise, vibration or harshness, although such failings were unthinkable to anybody inspired with Horch's ideals. Years before such a system was adopted by Citroën, the headlamps turned with the front wheels and a great central spotlight could be swung round by a linkage from a lever on the dashboard.

Bodies of exceptional beauty, in a broad Swabian style, were built on Horch chassis by Ahrens, Kathe, Glaeser, Lindner, Dietzsch, Erdmann & Rossi, and Wendler, but even a short-chassis two-door cabriolet weighed nearly 3 tons (3000kg). The engine, designed as it was to run for ever, produced only 120bhp, making the Horch a rather ponderous machine with a top speed of only 80mph (130km/h). A 7-seater long-chassis Pullman version weighed more than many trucks and was not much faster.

In the face of the mighty Maybach, and the 8-cylinder Grosser Mercedes which was based on an even bigger truck, the challenge from Horch wilted. The Auto Union combine's chief contribution rested in the machine tools which Horch laid in to produce the V12 engine and which proved invaluable when making Dr Porsche's extraordinary grand prix cars. The Horch V12 was the end of the road for the journeymen of Central Europe.

SPECIFICATION

Country of origin: Germany.

Manufacturer: Horch.

Model: 670.

Year: 1932.

Engine: V12 cylinder, side-valve, 6031cc.

Transmission: 4 forward ratios, live rear axle.

Body: Open or closed, 4, 5 or 7 seats.

Wheelbase: 136in (3450mm).

Length: 213in (5400mm).

Height: 66in (1676mm) to 78in (1981mm).

Width: 71in (1800mm).

Maximum speed: 81mph (130km/h).

The 1932 V12 was Packard's answer
to the Cadillac and Marmon V16s
— this glamorous convertible is bodied by Dietrich

The bizarre design of the headlamps
are worthy of note

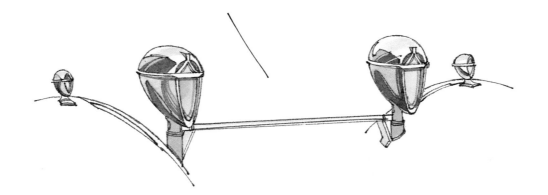

Packard bodies were so
luxurious they even had
apparatus for radio reception

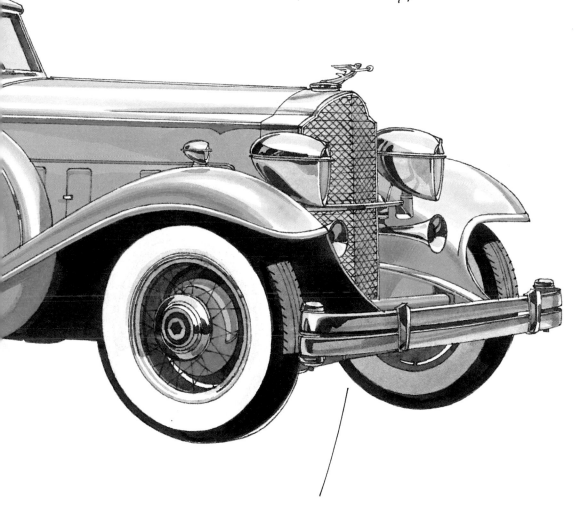

Beneath this elegant bonnet
was a V12 engine of 446 cu.in. and
150 bhp. It featured hydraulic valve
silencers and thermostatically controlled
automatic chokes plus a revolutionary
new electric fuel gauge

PACKARD V12

THE CARS AND aero engines produced by Packard achieved such a reputation for reliability and quality that the firm at one time gloried in the popular title of 'the American Rolls-Royce'. Their golden era started in 1915 when they introduced the world's first production V12 engine, based on a competition car built by the British firm Sunbeam. It had been sent to the United States when it could not be raced in war-torn Europe. From the start, Packard's early Twin Six cars, as they were called, oozed quality. The price of a bare chassis was higher than that of the most expensive complete Cadillac from General Motors.

The magnificent, sleek, silent and smooth-running Packards became the traditional transport of American Presidents after Warren Harding chose a 1921 model rather than a horse-drawn carriage to lead the first motorcade to the White House. The Packard Twin Six chassis also found much favour with undertakers seeking a stately hearse, and the early power unit gave rise to the famous Liberty engines of World War One. Later bulletproof Twin Sixes were especially popular with Franklin D. Roosevelt and elements of their construction were used in U.S. Secret Service vehicles. Naturally Al Capone had to have one so that he could go about his business during Prohibition without undue inconvenience. Armour-plated Twin Six chassis found their way to Venezuela to support General Juan Vincente Gomez, who was suffering local disturbances, and to mainland China for General Chiang Kai-shek's peace of mind at a time when the Manchurian warlord Chang Tso-Lin was spending a fortune having his Packard lined with special splinter-proof inlaid wood.

The Packard Twin Six was, naturally, very reliable. One, called El Toro, was probably the first car to cross the interior of Cuba. Despite some difficul-

ties with rarefied air, a Twin Six hauled its owner to the top of a 12,000ft (3657m) pass in the Andes so that he could photograph the statue of Christ marking the border between Argentina and Chile. Wealthy Americans were apt to consider such cars as a good investment when trying to compete with their neighbours. Belgium's Prince Eugène de Ligne drove a Twin Six across the Sahara Desert. King Alexander of Yugoslavia had about 50, some armed with heavy machine guns, distinguished by a crown on their radiator and green-and-white lights for clearing the traffic.

Other Twin Sixes had bizarre histories. A foreign lady with an unpronounceable name sent a favourite pink bedroom slipper to the factory at South Bend, Indiana, so that her Packard's upholstery could be matched to it and then changed her mind when, by the time the car was ready, the colour had gone out of fashion. Some Japanese mechanics went joyriding in the first Twin Six to reach the factory's new distributor in Tokyo. Finding the power and torque far greater than that of the locally built Son of Dat (Datsun) Austin Sevens, they lost control, ended up in the moat of the Imperial Palace and were fined for disturbing the goldfish!

Packard Twin Sixes forged an early entente with Russian aristocracy. Czar Nicholas sped along in one with swivelling skis in place of front wheels. His brother, Grand Duke Michael, fled the Bolsheviks in a Twin Six only to be killed when he stopped for dinner. The car survived and won one of the first motor races in Russia. Stalin was most impressed and bought one Twin Six after another until Packard stopped producing them. Nothing daunted, the Iron Man bought up the patterns and put them back into production as the Russian Zis State car for similarly placed comrades.

Later, during the Second World War, Packard

manufactured more 24-cylinder Rolls-Royce Merlin motors than the entire British aero engine industry. It was a case of the more cylinders the merrier for Packard, except in 1922 when they decided to out-general General Motors with a straight-eight. Their ace self-taught designer, Colonel Jesse G. Vincent, produced a magnificent vehicle which took Packard to the top of the American luxury car market. But there were customers who still hankered after a V12. When Cadillac came out with their V16, Packard had little option but to recreate the legendary Twin Six.

They realised that the market was limited during the days of the Depression, so they decided to set themselves apart from the rest of the American auto industry by resisting potentially ruinous annual model changes. Thus the first new Packards built in 1931 were called the Ninth Series, harking back to a glorious past when the Twin Six had been changed every year between 1915 and 1922. The new Twin Six was an especially significant motor car in that, although produced only in small numbers, it had many brand-new features. These appeared on lesser Packards of the Ninth Series, which sold by the thousand.

The Twin Six pioneered Packard's famous vee-shaped radiator; the movement of massive spring-loaded bumpers was damped by oil to iron out unwanted chassis flexing; the braking system for this heavy car was boosted by a vacuum servo; the aluminium-headed engine was given dual down-draught carburettors with thermostatically controlled automatic chokes, and the dashboard, which contained an electric fuel gauge, would soon receive apparatus for radio reception.

Initially the new Twin Six was available only with coachwork by Dietrich in four styles, a Sport Phaeton, a Fixed-head Coupé, a Convertible Coupé and a Convertible Sedan, all vastly over-priced at between $6,500-$7,000 (£4,350-£4,650). Demand for these cars with rakish vee-shaped windscreens, short scuttles and long bonnets was so slow that the 1932 production run did not sell out until 1934, proving the wisdom of Packard's policy of avoiding annual model changes. This also meant, of course, that they did not have to keep any particular model in production for a whole year, being able to introduce a new series whenever they felt the timing to be right.

As new modifications were introduced the Twin Six went to a Seventeenth Series before bowing out for World War Two. The last model made for President Roosevelt had bodywork and windows proof against peppering by heavy machine-gun bullets, and a foldaway hood so strong that, when erected, it could shield the occupant from a direct hit by a grenade dropped from as high as 250 feet (76m). Packard had thought of everything even if potential assassins had not.

SPECIFICATION

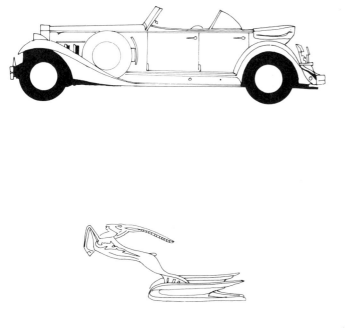

Country of origin: United States of America.

Manufacturer: Packard.

Model: Twin Six.

Year: 1932.

Engine: V12 cylinder, side-valve, 7297cc.

Transmission: 3 forward ratios, live rear axle.

Body: Open, 4 seats.

Wheelbase: 120in (3048mm).

Length: 215in (5461mm).

Height: 65in (1651mm).

Width: 74in (1880mm).

Maximum speed: 93mph (150km/h).

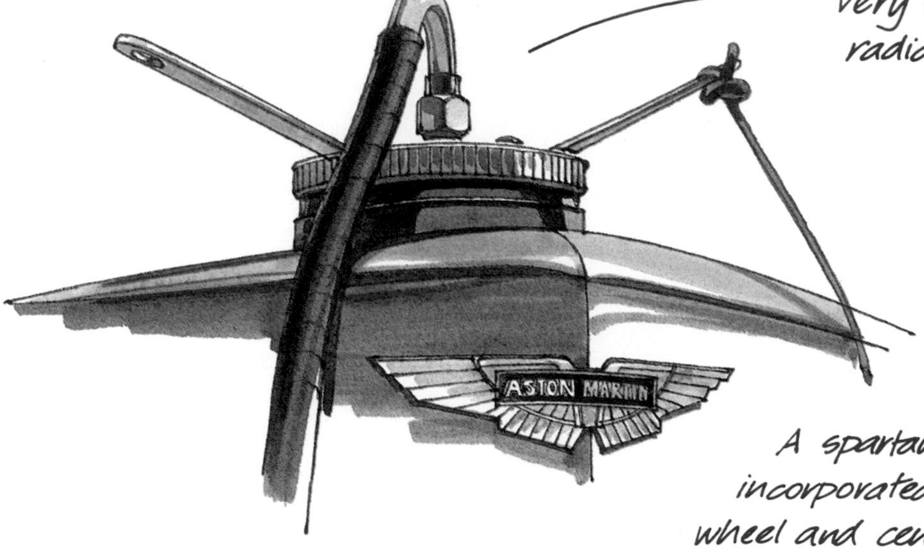

Very simple
radiator overflow

A spartan cockpit
incorporated a large steering
wheel and central
accelerator pedal

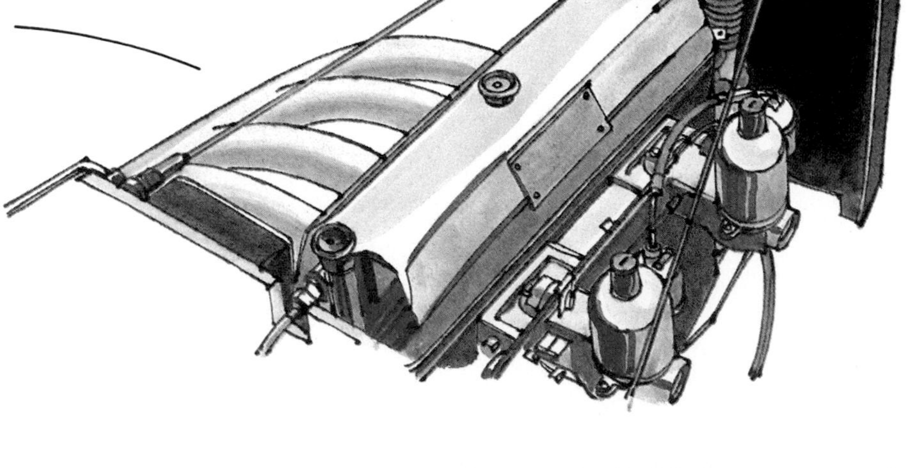

1495cc overhead camshaft engine
had dry sump lubrication and
a crossflow head, with twin
SU carburettors

ASTON MARTIN

ASTON MARTIN ULSTER

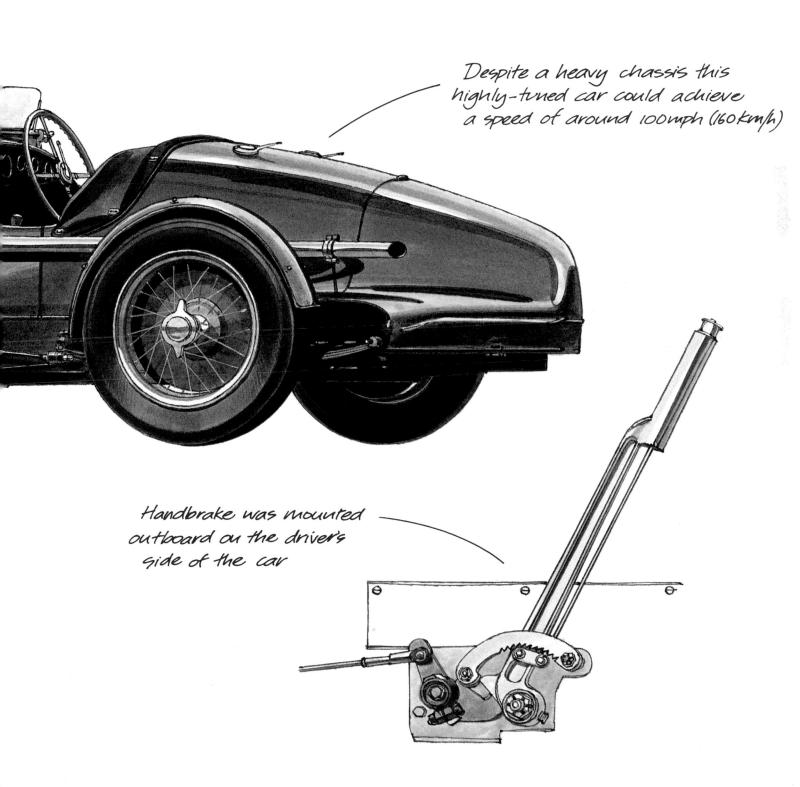

Despite a heavy chassis this highly-tuned car could achieve a speed of around 100mph (160km/h)

Handbrake was mounted outboard on the driver's side of the car

ASTON MARTINS HAVE always been rather heavy machines and, with the odd exception, of such pleasing proportions and obviously high performance that the pre-war types have been likened to Bugattis and the post-war to Ferraris. But the one quality that has always distinguished the marque is that Aston Martins are so typically English.

The early cars varied in detail specification, but one stood far above the rest: the Ulster, which took its name from the venue of Britain's oldest road race, the Tourist Trophy. Only 21 of these fabulous machines were produced for customers between 1934 and 1935, with a handful of others for the works team to race.

Aston Martin owed its existence to competition and the enthusiasm of two former racing cyclists, Robert Bamford and Lionel Martin, who progressed independently to classic trials and hill climbs in small Singer sports cars soon after the First World War. Martin, an archetypal English sporting gentleman, was always the more spectacular, forcing his machine to the very limit of its power – so much so that he often had engine trouble. It was typical of Martin that when his Singer finally gave up the ghost at the bottom of Beggar's Roost on the English equivalent of the Monte Carlo Rally, the Land's End Trial, he should dismount, change his socks – he had been on the road for hours – don his Old Etonian tie, brush himself down and saunter off to the nearest village for technical assistance.

Bamford, who built bespoke mechanical devices, was just the man to help. Between them, Bamford and Martin resolved to build their own car, incorporating all the good qualities of the Singer, notably its nimble handling, and hopefully avoiding its faults,

chiefly its lack of reliability. But, most important, their new machine had to be a road car which could also be raced. It took its name, Aston Martin, from Martin's early exploits with a Singer at the Aston Clinton hill climb in Buckinghamshire. It was there that the crowd of enthusiasts would roll up, each with a different machine, do their best, and then celebrate with a good party afterwards.

Martin was a gregarious fellow with many sporting friends, among whom were the ever-cheery Bertie Kensington Moir, driver of a big Straker-Squire, Count Louis Zborowski, very rich, very temperamental and very Polish, and Clive Gallop, steeped in the heroic age of French racing, who liked to be called Gallo. Inevitably, Bamford and Martin began building cars for men like these and by 1921, no meeting at the national racetrack, Brooklands – 'built for the good of the nation' – was complete without Aston Martins in the paddock. They were never quite as fast as the chief competition, built by A.C., because they were really intended for use on the road and weighed more than spartan track cars of the day. In any case, Martin was a big chap and liked a sturdy chassis beneath him. But despite their weight, and like their prime mover, Astons could always be relied upon to put on a good performance. And in a typically English manner, the 'Aston boys' felt that it was somehow unsporting to derive a profit from their venture. It was hardly surprising the firm nearly went bust in 1925.

The general feeling was that there should always be a place for such a marque in Britain, so it was revived in 1926 by two society enthusiasts Lord Charnwood and the Hon John Benson. They certainly brought in the right managing director too, a man who will always be remembered as the 'Father of Aston Martin,' Augustus Cesari Bertelli. He was a gifted Italian mechanic who had ridden with the legendary Felice Nazzaro, but now lived in Wales.

Bertelli was far more than a managing director. He represented everything that Aston Martin stood for to a wealthy and often aristocratic clientèle by acting more in the manner of a top horse trainer. Bertelli was able to explain the advanced design of this exclusive and so proudly English sporting car, in the most disarmingly simple manner, then provide immaculate service to keep it running. To achieve such ends, Bertelli became not only designer, salesman and service manager, but test driver too, a role which he filled with distinction.

His elder brother Enrico built bodywork and helped on the drawing board and Bertelli was able to turn the Aston Martin works at Feltham, Middlesex, into a reasonably commercial enterprise. And the Bertellis' good humour and tact stood them in good stead as customers burst in to address Enrico as Harry and slap the managing director on the back with a hearty 'Bertie, old chap!'

Needless to say, such customers entered all the best races and Bertelli was able to offer just what they wanted: almost limitless variations on the 1½-litre four-cylinder engine and chassis that gave Aston Martins their character. This meant that the cars had to be capable not only of everyday road work, but competitions as diverse as the Le Mans 24-hour race, the Brooklands Double-12, the Six Hour blind on the same rough concrete track, the Tourist Trophy round the tortuous back roads of Northern Ireland, the Belgian 24-hour race at Spa and the Mille Miglia round Italy. The main problem which arose was that Aston Martins were always a bit slow off the mark because they had to be strong enough to withstand such treatment year after year.

The Ulster became the greatest of the early Astons, not only because it was the last and most highly developed of the original 1.5-litre machines, but because it was the closest to an outright racing car. For a small car weighing nearly one ton (1016kg), it displayed a remarkable turn of speed thanks to its highly tuned and beautifully built overhead camshaft dry-sump engine. Everything about it reflected its thoroughbred lineage, from the central accelerator pedal which made the racing driver's art of operating the throttle with his toe and the brakes with his heel so much easier, to the screaming straight-cut gears and blaring exhaust running outside the slim body, the sides of which were cut away to make way for flailing elbows in some hectic dice.

All great things come to an end, and Bertelli retired in 1936. From then on Aston Martin lurched from one financial crisis to the next, frequently surviving thanks only to the heroic efforts of an enthusiastic English clientèle.

SPECIFICATION

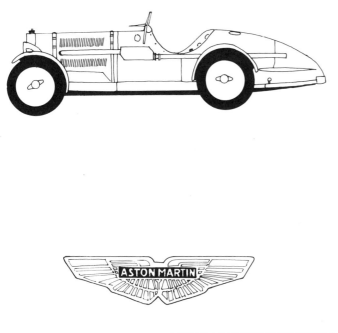

Country of origin: Great Britain.

Manufacturer: Aston Martin.

Model: Ulster.

Year: 1935.

Engine: 4-cylinder in-line, overhead camshaft, 1495cc.

Transmission: 4 forward ratios, live rear axle.

Body: Open, 2 seats.

Wheelbase: 103in (2616mm).

Length: 138in (3505mm).

Height: 55in (1397mm).

Width: 64in (1626mm).

Maximum speed: 100mph (161km/h).

The 851 Boat-tailed Speedster
boasted a Duesenberg-designed
supercharger, 150 bhp
and a top speed
in excess of
100mph (160km/h)

V12 Boat-tailed Speedster.
160 bhp at 3500 rpm. This model
sold for as little as $1600 (£1050)

AUBURN BOAT-TAILED SPEEDSTER

Tiny hood required two people to remove and stow

Radiator of the 851.
This model was timed
at 103mph (166km/h),
the 'Flying Mile'

AUBURN BOAT-TAILED SPEEDSTER

Like all Auburns, the boat-tailed Speedster amounted to a triumph of styling over specification, but nobody who bought one cared a dime that a Stutz was faster: Auburns always *looked* faster – much to their owners' delight – and cost a lot less, which those same owners were reluctant to reveal. Thus, when all was said and done, Auburns gained a reputation for being classics of the con man's art. As such they were the solid rock on which Errett Lobban Cord's business empire was founded.

The Auburn Automobile Company was almost on its last legs when Cord fell over it in 1924 – or when Auburn tripped over Cord. Exactly which version is the accurate description of how they came into contact has never been established, but the result was the same. Cord, whose assets had risen from $45 (£30) in 1919 to around $100,000 (£67,000) five years later, through inspired car salesmanship in California, sold himself to the moribund Auburn company with the line that only he knew how to make money from their stocks of largely unsaleable old-fashioned cars. Neither party parted with any money at this stage.

Cord's first action as general manager was to tart up 700 outdated Auburns parked behind the factory, with nickel plating that reeked of good taste, and flashy paintwork which reflected the mood of young America – a brash class of hard-working folk with an obviously disposable income, a class which the conservative Auburn management had failed to attract. Result: Cord whipped in half a million dollars in his first year, largely from sales of cars that nobody had previously wanted. He doubled sales in the next year, and again the following year, although profits were a mere million dollars then because Auburn were having to make cars again. Cord also managed to impose himself as company president.

He then raised money by methods which were completely in tune with the fast-buck method of doing business on the American stock market of the mid-1920s. As stocks rose with news of huge profits, Cord sold off large blocks to rake in other stocks and shares, triggering, first, a drop in the prices of his own stocks, and at the same time a rise in the prices of the ones he took in part exchange. The process was then reversed and repeated, buying back his original stock at rock-bottom prices, and using the surplus to gain control of other companies, such as Duesenberg and Lycoming. Small wonder that Wall Street crashed in 1929, largely as a result of the then quite legal activities of men like Cord.

As car sales plunged in the aftermath of the Crash, Cord cut back the Auburn range, stifled development costs, slashed profits to the bone, and survived with a V-shaped sales graph of 22,000 in 1929, 14,000 in 1930 and 32,000 in 1931. The profit margin, however, remained low, which inspired Cord to go for bust with cars that made more money.

Cadillac, Packard and Pierce-Arrow were making a small fortune from every one of the few V12-cylinder cars they could sell, so Cord wanted one, too, figuring that, as the best car salesman in America, and probably the world, he could solve the minor problem of getting rid of such exotic machinery. Or at least machinery which looked exotic. So Lycoming had to jump to it and produce a cheap V12, which, to their credit, was powerful enough on 391 cubic inches, or 6.4 litres, to propel Auburn's old straight-eight chassis at more than 100mph (160km/h).

Sad to say, few people wanted a V12 during such austere days, even if it cost a third of the price of its competitors and had rakish Speedster bodywork. Now the sales graph went straight down from less than 8000 in 1932 to round off at 4703 in 1934. Cord, in trouble over his share dealings, took refuge in England, leaving Harold Ames, his hard-working associate at Duesenberg, in effective control.

When faced with such adversity in the showroom, Ames could only take a leaf out of the Cord manual of salesmanship, adding a touch of Duesenberg's desirability. He roped in Duesenberg's master stylist Gordon Buehrig to revamp the Speedster with the old Lycoming straight-eight in place of the hard-to-sell V12. The new Auburn still had to perform well, however, so he also called in ace engineer Augie Duesenberg to supercharge it, reckoning that the scream of such a device would make a good sales pitch.

Buehrig, *enfant terrible* of American styling, worked wonders in adapting a batch of 100 redundant V12 Speedster bodies, designed by Cord L-29 bodyman Al Leamy. Using his earlier Duesenberg SJ Speedster as inspiration, Buehrig cut off the back and substituted a boat-tail shape, which could be made quickly and cheaply, and hopefully see Auburn through their crisis. He used new front and rear wings to help disguise the coachwork's origins, safe in the knowledge that the old fenders were likely to be in the heaviest demand for repairs to damaged '33 models. A new radiator grille, chrome sidewinder exhausts like those of a Mercedes SSK, and the Speedster's spirit of Auburn bonnet motif repeated on the body sides, completed his cut-price package.

Augie Duesenberg, meanwhile, had managed to coax 150bhp out of the venerable 115bhp straight-eight, achieving the necessary performance partly because his truck-style supercharger blew through enough mixture and partly because it did so at less pressure than Auburn's salesman wanted and claimed, pressure which would have blown the top off the old Lycoming. Thus Auburn were saved again – for the time being – by the genius of others.

There was technical innovation too beneath Buehrig's glamorous tail. The use of a Columbia rear axle, the dual ratios of which were achieved by interposing an epicyclic gear train between axle and crown wheel, reflected the needs of another part of Cord's struggling empire. It gave the Auburn, with its conventional three-speed gearbox, six forward ratios and the ability to cruise at 60mph (97km/h) on just 2250rpm in almost complete mechanical silence – a feat which far larger rivals, such as General Motors, had been trying to achieve for years on budgets many times greater. To add to its list of achievements, this backs-to-the-wall production became the first fully-equipped American production car to average more than 100mph (160km/h) for half a day.

But it was not enough to save E. L. Cord, deep in trouble over shares. He sold out, while Buehrig, ironically, went on to design the unforgettable coffin-nosed Cord.

SPECIFICATION

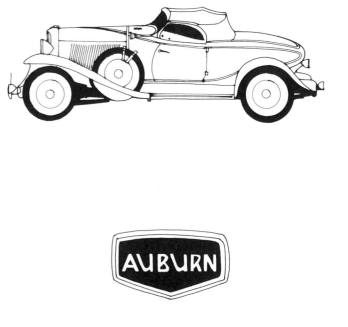

Country of origin: United States of America.

Manufacturer: Auburn.

Model: Boat-tailed Speedster.

Year: 1935.

Engine: 8-cylinder in-line, side-valve, 4585cc supercharged.

Transmission: 3 forward ratios, live rear axle.

Body: Open, 2 seats.

Wheelbase: 127in (3226mm).

Length: 194in (4938mm).

Height: 60in (1524mm).

Width: 72in (1816mm).

Maximum speed: 103mph (166km/h).

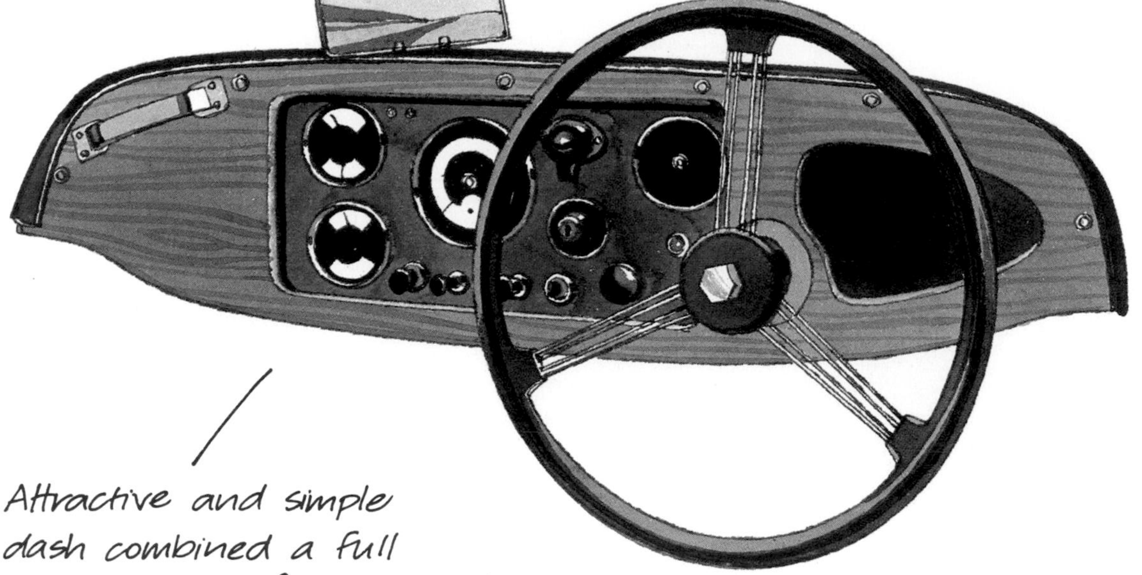

Attractive and simple
dash combined a full
complement of instruments
including tachometer

The 4/4 was the first
four-wheel Morgan sports
car and was soon developed
to offer an alternative
drophead coupé body style
as illustrated

Louvred bonnet concealed
1122cc Coventry Climax engine
that produced 34bhp.
    Later models had a 1276cc
    O.H.V. Standard engine
    of 40bhp

Twin spare wheels
were carried,
secured by an
aluminium bracket

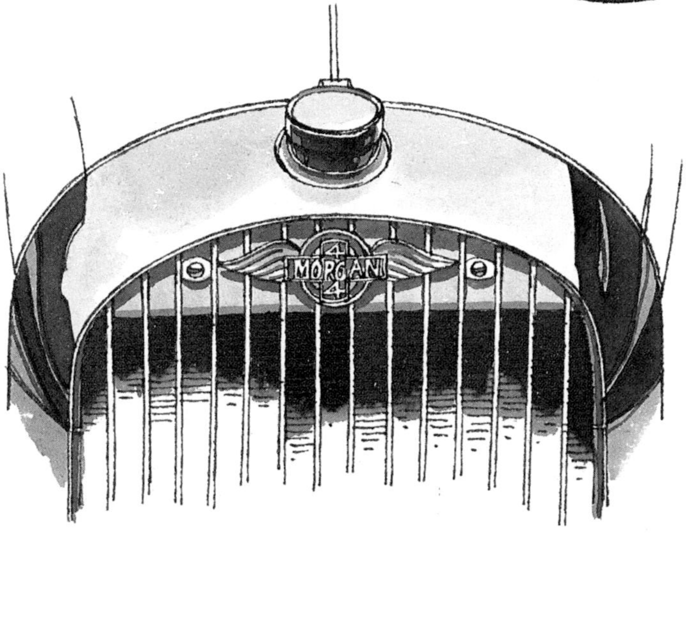

Classic flat radiator of the
4/4 with winged Morgan
emblem. The radiator shell
was hand-made in 3 pieces

MORGAN
4 4

MORGAN 4/4

Bᴿɪᴛɪꜱʜ Mᴏʀɢᴀɴꜱ ʜᴀᴠᴇ remained in production largely unaltered for 50 years . . . longer than any other car in the world. Yet hardly any two of the 15,000 or so four-wheeled Morgans built since 1936 are exactly alike. This is because they have all been built by hand as traditional sports cars with a body, chassis and suspension dating from the early part of the century. The body panels, in particular, have to be 'fettled' by hand for the best fit, and can be varied to meet the special needs of a customer wanting two, or maybe four, seats. As a result, with varying levels of trim, each Morgan is a little different from the next, making it a most appealing car to the individualist.

One of the basic features which has hardly changed since the first glorious flat-radiator model in 1936 is the chassis itself. It is laid out like a ladder with independent front suspension featuring sliding pillars on which the wheels can be steered. This system, which amounts to a doubling-up of a motor cycle's front suspension, dates back to 1910 when the first three-wheeled Morgans were produced as rivals to a motor cycle and sidecar. The system may be as old as the motor industry, but it still works exceptionally well with modern tyres, which rely on being kept as near vertical as possible to the road surface. The Morgan's rear suspension, the well-tried layout using a live axle mounted on half-elliptic springs, is even older, having first been used on farm carts. Yet it keeps the wheels upright, and – with modern rubberware – contributes to excellent roadholding. Morgans are full of surprises!

As a small family firm producing around 10 cars a week from their original headquarters in Malvern, Worcestershire, Morgan have always had to rely on the products of larger companies for items which are expensive to develop, like engines. Using the cheap basic components from mass-produced sports or saloon cars has also fitted in well with their philosophy of producing a highly individual open car at a very competitive price. Such ideals have also proved exceptionally good for business, with customers waiting as long as six years for a new Morgan. At other times, when the demand for 'new antiques' has fallen, the factory has been glad that its existence has never been endangered by having to finance a stockpile of Morgans.

High performance has always been of paramount importance to Morgan's customers. The owners of the earliest four-wheel cars were mostly concerned with reliability trials, a pre-war form of rallying. These trials, usually held on unsurfaced roads deep in the heart of England, were of great importance because there was little circuit racing in Britain before the war. This meant that the new four-wheeled Morgans had to have as good a performance as the very light three-wheelers powered by potent motor-cycle engines. So the mundane Ford engine used in the 1935 prototype, called the 4/4, because it four cylinders and four wheels, was replaced by a proprietary Coventry Climax unit used by several other manufacturers at the time, and a gearbox made by Meadows. This was mounted separately, well back in the frame for better balance, with more weight being concentrated over the rear axle by fitting twin spare wheels. These wheels were equipped with knobbly tyres which replaced the normal rubber when the Morgan needed more grip in a trial. Such tyres made a mess of the 'road', so they were banned in 1938, but the habit of carrying two spare wheels on a Morgan persisted for years to provide better traction by weighing down the driven wheels.

Apart from starring in the classic trials, such as the London-to-Land's End, a forerunner of the Monte Carlo Rally, Morgans also managed to win Britain's Royal Automobile Club Rally three times in succession from 1937. They also did well in Britain's oldest race, the Tourist Trophy, held in Northern Ireland,

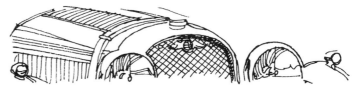

where roads could be closed for such events. Racing Morgans were duly equipped with a rakish light-weight tail carrying only one spare wheel to save weight. It was in this form that a wealthy young lady, Miss Prudence M. Fawcett, decided to use a 4/4 to take part in her first race, the Le Mans 24-hour! You needed no qualifications to enter this classic event in 1938 . . . but despite her lack of experience, Miss Fawcett's Morgan proved so reliable when driven steadily that she took 13th place as faster and more exotic racing cars fell by the wayside. Sadly, it was Miss Fawcett's last race and she hasn't been heard of since.

Morgans carried on almost unchanged, however, except that they acquired a different engine, from Standard, and in 1939 a Moss gearbox. These more readily available units stayed with Morgan until Standard increased the capacity from 1.3 litres to 2 litres in 1950, after which the Morgan 4/4 could be bought with either a small Ford Anglia engine or Standard's saloon-car motor. The 2-litre Standard unit was subsequently developed into a more powerful sports version which went into a Morgan called the Plus 4.

The big four-cylinder engine was rugged in the extreme, featuring in the Ferguson light tractor, and helping to maintain Morgan's image of producing thoroughly dependable basic sports cars. The traditional nose had to be remodelled in 1953 to incorporate a curved radiator cowling and recessed head-lamps as supplies of the earlier items became obsolete. Curved noses and concealed radiators or not, Morgans continued to win rallies in the 1950s, partly because of their good handling, partly because they were light with no frills, and partly because they were so strong.

A lot of power could be extracted from the Standard engine, so much so that tuning wizard Chris Lawrence took his Plus 4 model to another 13th place at Le Mans in 1962. It was then decided that the Morgan chassis might benefit from a more aerodynamic body, and three racing versions, called the SLR, were built with fixed-head bodywork. A production version called the Plus 4 Plus was marketed. But these cars were never very successful and since then the Morgan family has stuck to the principle that almost anything can change under the skin so long as a Morgan looks like a Morgan.

Such changes were never more dramatic than when the Rover 3.5-litre V8 engine was adopted for a 125mph (200km/h) top model, the Plus 8 in 1968, along with Ford's four-cylinder Cortina engine in the 4/4 when the Standard unit went out of production. More recently the Ford engine has been supplemented by Fiat's 2-litre twin cam unit to resurrect the Plus 4 model name. In this way Morgans have been able to carry on almost unchanged . . . still with the founder's son, Peter Morgan, at the helm.

SPECIFICATION

Country of origin: Great Britain.

Manufacturer: Morgan.

Model: 4/4.

Year: 1936.

Engine: Coventry Climax, 4-cylinder in-line, overhead inlet, side exhaust, 1122cc.

Transmission: Meadows four ratios, live rear axle.

Body: Open, 2 seats.

Wheelbase: 92in (2336mm).

Length: 140in (3556mm).

Height: 49in (1245mm) hood erect.

Width: 54in (1372mm).

Maximum speed: 75mph (121km/h).

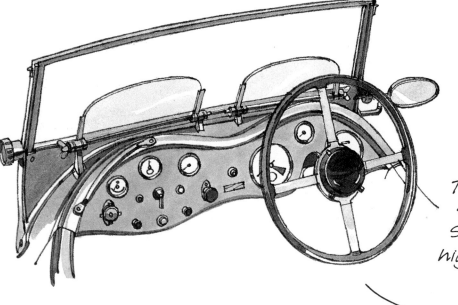

Steel chassis was clothed with an alloy body on ash framing

The dashboard and steering wheel of the SS100 were typical of high quality pre-War sports cars

JAGUAR SS100

Beautiful body was designed by William Lyons.
This car is the 3.5-litre version — capable
of 100mph (160km/h)

Spare wheel was mounted
externally on slab fuel tank

JAGUAR SS100

THE BRITISH FIRM of Jaguar sprang from small beginnings and went from building bodies for motor cycle sidecars in a shed by the sea at Blackpool to their present position as builders of what many people claim to be the 'Best Car in the World'. Whether or not the present Jaguars really deserve that title, there is no doubt that few other cars can match their renowned grace, space and pace. It should also be realised that they have almost always been the products of one master stylist, the late Sir William Lyons. His first bodies in 1920 adopted the name Swallow, that of a bird with all the grace and pace in the world. Lyons invariably took inspiration from wildlife when creating a message in metal.

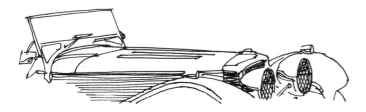

Not only was he able to inspire others to carve his forms in wood, so that they could be copied in metal, but he was a hard-headed businessman. He knew how to cut corners to save money in production and how to save his firm when all around were foundering. When the introduction of the Austin Seven sounded the death knell for mass-produced motorcycle combinations, Lyons changed the course of his business to building bodies on the Austin Seven's chassis. Others tried the same approach, but their bodies still looked like those of the primitive motorcycle sidecars. The bodies designed by Lyons certainly did not. His Swallow bodywork was soon recognised not only as being the most stylish available on a small car, but also as offering the best value in a fickle market where people would pay a high premium for an Austin Seven which looked different from that of their neighbour.

Lyons was keen to hedge his bets lest Austin should start making their own special bodies at extra cost, and by virtue of the economies of a larger-scale operation, put him out of business. He also felt frustration at having to conform to the dictates of others over issues such as dimensions, so he did a deal with the Standard Motor Company to make special powered chassis for Swallow bodies. These formed the basis for the cars called SS for Swallow Standard, Standard Swallow, Swallow Special or Standard Special; exactly which combination Lyons would not reveal.

The venture proved so successful that Lyons had to move his works to Coventry, in the industrial Midlands of England, where there was more skilled labour. But already people jealous of the success of SS sniped that the cars were not nearly as fast as they looked. Lyons did not want to gain a reputation for producing cars which, when put to the test, performed no better than the cheaper models on which they were based, so he hired the brilliant tuning expert, Harry Weslake, to extract more power from the stolid Standard engine. Weslake worked wonders to raise the output of a 2.5-litre version of this engine from 70bhp to 105, with 125bhp from an enlarged 3.5-litre edition!

Lyons then went on to manufacture a short-wheelbase version of his SS1 saloon, with the lighter open bodywork of a two-seater sports car, to be called the SS90 because it was good for 90mph (145km/h). As ever, his styling was extraordinarily good, resulting in one of the most spectacular sports cars built before the 1939-45 war. Significantly it was also the cheapest in its class.

But his main business came from building sporting saloon cars, so the new engines were used in his bigger luxury cars too. These elegant saloons were every bit as attractive as the sports cars. Lyons felt, quite naturally, that they deserved a new name, particularly as he had just broken up with his partner, William Walmsley, with whom he had

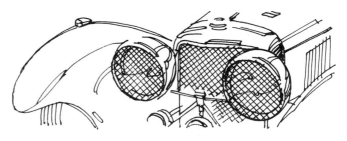

started in business. Now that Lyons was alone, he called in his advertising agents and asked them to draw up a list of names from the animal world which would represent the grace and power he was trying to convey. The autocratic Lyons then picked one word from the list, thanked his agents, and for ever called his cars, simply, Jaguars. In time they became so well-known that today there are people who do not initially associate the name of the car with that of a relatively obscure South American jungle cat.

But it needed only the 3.5-litre engine to be transferred to the short-chassis open two-seater for the SS100 – which did 100mph (160km/h) quite easily – to become one of the most desirable pre-war sports cars. There was nothing to match its elegance and performance, even at twice the price.

Lyons was happy to keep this classic in relatively short supply, however, because the larger saloon cars, with more bodywork, made more money. He did not raise the price of the sports car to what the market might have paid for it, though, because he did not want to divorce it from his saloon cars, reasoning that a high price would make it seem very special and quite different from his normal product. The publicity gained from its successes in competition was also more than welcome on the sales front, virtually killing rival sporting saloons produced by the far bigger manufacturer, M.G.

By the end of 1938, two years after the SS100

Jaguar had been introduced, production was running at more than 5000 cars a year, of which only a few hundred were sports cars – giving them an even more exclusive appeal.

The reputation was heightened by the exploits of works-sponsored examples driven in rallies by journalist Tommy Wisdom – who was certainly good for publicity! – and magistrate Sammy Newsome. Soon their favourite SS100 was stripped for track work and became known as Old Number Eight, after its chassis plate, the registration plate number by which it would normally have been known in England having disappeared in the effort to lose weight.

These SS Jaguars continued in production until war was declared in 1939, and when peace returned in 1945, the initials SS had sinister overtones. So the letters were dropped for all Lyons's cars produced after the war. Austerity was the order of the day, and supplies of steel were short, so his range of Jaguars – hardly altered from SS saloons sold pre-war – did not include the fabulous SS100.

But one escaped from the factory, having been assembled from spare parts which had survived the hostilities. It was driven by Lyons's son-in-law, Jaguar dealer Ian Appleyard, with the master-designer's daughter, Pat, to numerous victories in international rallies, giving the lie to any lingering claims that the first Jaguars did not perform as well as they looked.

SPECIFICATION

Country of origin: Great Britain.

Manufacturer: S.S. Cars.

Model: Jaguar 100.

Year: 1936.

Engine: 6-cylinder in-line, overhead valve, 3485cc.

Transmission: 4 forward ratios, live rear axle.

Body: Open, 2 seats.

Wheelbase: 104in (2642mm).

Length: 153in (3886mm).

Height: 56in (1422mm) hood erect.

Width: 63in (1600mm).

Maximum speed: 101mph (163km/h).

'V' radiator was exciting, but was also the first Bugatti radiator not to be nickel-silver plated

BUGATTI T57SC ATLANTIC

Factory designed and produced body was fitted to the short wheelbase chassis — it was built in two halves then rivetted together

The 57SC had a supercharged engine that would propel the car at 112 mph (180 km/h)

BUGATTI T57SC ATLANTIC

ONLY THREE EXAMPLES of the Atlantic coupé, Bugatti's most exotic production, were made, but they have all survived. They were essentially the creation of Jean Bugatti, the influence of his father Ettore having waned by the time the first Type 57 chassis was laid down in 1934. In contrast to his father's policy of offering a variety of models, Type 57 Bugattis were all basically the same. But they were produced in varying states of tune with widely differing bodywork, so that Type 57s ranged from relatively sedate saloons to sports-racing cars. This standardisation of parts made them more profitable to produce, individual attraction being retained by fitting some chassis with the most extraordinary coachwork, of which the Atlantic coupé was the greatest.

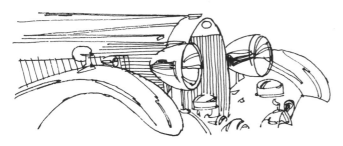

The first Type 57, later known as the Normale, was also far more commercial in its appeal than many earlier Bugattis because the engine was designed primarily for flexibility rather than outright power. This made the Normale especially easy to drive, avoiding the frequent gear changes needed with more highly tuned machinery. Nevertheless, its superb 3.3-litre straight eight-cylinder twin overhead cam-shaft engine gave it enough power to outperform most other cars on the road.

This power unit, with a one-piece cylinder block like that of the Type 59 racing car, was mated directly to the gearbox through a single-plate clutch, for the first time in a Bugatti. Helical constant-mesh gears were favoured for silence of operation with sliding 'dog' clutches for easy engagement. Some cars were fitted with Cotal electro-mechanical gearboxes, which made them even simpler to drive. The sturdy rear axle from the Type 46 touring model was soon made a standard fitting for silence of operation.

Bugatti also managed to make the Type 57 more profitable by substituting a plated radiator shell for the superb nickel-silver honeycomb radiator used on all their previous road cars. Happily, the new V-shaped grille was at least as good-looking, if not better, than the outmoded flat radiator. Bugatti also offered the Type 57 for the first time with bodywork fitted at the factory, rather than just as a rolling chassis which was then sent to a coachbuilder to have its body fitted. Specialist coachworks, such as Gang-loff, continued to offer drop-head coupé bodywork on the Type 57 chassis, called the Stelvio, as Bugatti built a variety of bodies named Galibier, Ventoux, Atalante, Aravis, Surbaisse and ultimately, Atlantic.

Most of the early production was made up of standard chassis, with a type 57S model being introduced in 1936. This used a more powerful high-compression engine, dry-sump lubrication, a Scintilla competition magneto and twin-plate racing clutch in a lighter short-wheelbase chassis which was lowered to improve the handling by passing the rear axle through holes in the side rails. When fitted with sporting bodywork, these long low cars were fast enough and handled sufficiently well to attract customers like the Land Speed record holder, Sir Malcolm Campbell. He rated his Type 57S as the best sports car in the world.

Inevitably, in 1936, a Type 57 was fitted with a supercharger for even better performance, being known as the Type 57C (for compressor). The Normale Type 57 could reach around 95mph (150km/h), according to the weight of bodywork, but the Type 57C was good for 112mph (180km/h). The ultimate combination was reached at the same time when the supercharged engine was fitted to the short-wheelbase chassis for the Type 57SC.

Perhaps conscious that these Bugattis were no longer bespoke motor cars, the factory went overboard with their special bodywork. If exotic is taken to mean strange and bizarre, few cars could match an Atalante coupé in fixed-head or convertible form, or a Surbaisse roadster with all-enclosed wheels. But the most extraordinary was the Atlantic two-seater fixed-head coupé with typically low sweeping lines and panels arranged so that the body could be assembled in two halves, then riveted together on a central spine that made it look like a creature from another world.

Ettore Bugatti's dream of a feudal empire ended in 1936, however, as French workers achieved revolutionary powers and he had to retreat from Molsheim, in Alsace, to Paris, leaving his son Jean to run the operation. Jean was not only an excellent designer, but also a very good driver. With the fortunes of the family firm in mind, Ettore Bugatti would not let him race and Jean had to content himself with breaking records for rail travel with train engines designed by his father, and testing their racing cars on the road. It was during one of these test sessions that he died, crashing beside a typically French tree-lined road near Molsheim in 1939, robbing the country of one of its most talented designers.

The elder Bugatti – who designed all manner of objects from surgical instruments to aeroplane engines, from bicycles to boats, from special locks on the solid oak doors of his factory to its own electricity generating plant, and filled his museum with the sculptures of his dead brother Rembrandt – lived on. As war broke out and the German Army marched into France, he lost his pride and joy, the factory which was always swept as clean as a clinic, with rank upon rank of the best and most expensive machine tools in the world.

When the war was over, despite being Italian and technically a enemy national, he petitioned for its return. He was successful because the French had grown to regard Bugattis as their national car and the engines originally intended for his magnificent Royale saloon had given sterling service in railcars. But Bugatti was old, money was short, and death overtook him in 1947 before four new prototypes could be completed. His surviving son, Roland, tried to revive the Type 57 as the Type 101 with Gangloff coachwork four years later, but had to admit financial defeat, further efforts to create a grand prix car failing for similar reasons in 1956.

Molsheim soldiered on, servicing railcar engines, with nearby textile manufacturers, the Schlumpf brothers, buying up every available Bugatti, including examples from Le Patron's museum. Then, they too were ousted by the workers and the Schlumpf Collection was taken over as the Musée Nationale de l'Automobile. But one model escaped . . . the fabulous Atlantic. They are all in private hands on either side of the Atlantic.

SPECIFICATION

Country of origin: France.

Manufacturer: Bugatti.

Model: Type 57SC Atlantic.

Year: 1937.

Engine: 8-cylinder in-line, twin overhead camshaft, 3250cc supercharged.

Transmission: 4 forward ratios, live rear axle.

Body: Fixed-head coupé, 2 seats.

Wheelbase: 118in (2985mm).

Length: 199in (5069mm).

Height: 50in (1270mm).

Width: 61in (1550mm).

Maximum speed: 125mph (201km/h).

4.4-litre V12 engine was designed by
W.O. Bentley and was capable of
propelling the car at 103 mph (165 km/h)

Wire wheels on this car were covered by the
then popular easy-clean 'Ace' wheel discs

The V12 Rapides were all built on short (10ft 4in / 3150mm)
chassis and had Lagonda-built coachwork —
they were some 3cwt (152kg) lighter
than the standard V12 saloon

LAGONDA V12

THE STORY OF how the Lagonda came by its name is part of a chapter of American history. Where the Shawnee tribe once hunted in the lush woods along the banks of the Ohio river, white settlers came and forced them off their land. All that remained of the Shawnee was their name for a peculiar twisting tributary of the Ohio which they called Ough Ohonda – or Buck's Horns – because that's what its network of streams most resembled. Soon French traders had corrupted the name to La Ohonda, and native Americans who followed called it Lagonda. The name was then adopted for the area surrounding the Buck's Horns, populated by families like that of river trader Horace Gunn. The densely wooded banks of the Lagonda gave way to the factories of Springfield where a boy named Wilbur Adams Gunn was born in 1859 and later apprenticed in the local Singer sewing machine works. It was there that he gained an uncommonly good grounding in the art of making anything mechanical although his chief interest lay in operatic singing!

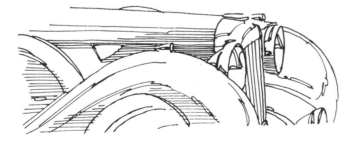

No sooner had Gunn completed his apprenticeship than his youthful marriage collapsed, so he set sail for pastures new, to Europe, with every intention of becoming an opera singer rather than just a sewing machine mechanic. Somehow he landed on the banks of the River Thames at Staines, west of London, and in the arms of a very English lady called Constance, who bred bulldogs and tolerated her new husband's interest in things mechanical. With Constance by his side, the young Gunn became extremely English in his attitudes, in fact, more English than the English themselves, in the manner of many converts. But it seems that he left part of his heart by a river far away. He called the marvellous new machines that his wife financed, Lagondas.

They started off as motor cycles, built in a works set up in the grounds of their riverside home. These Lagondas were extremely well made, one becoming famous as the Mercedes of Motor-Cycling when Gunn rode it to a gold medal as the only finisher within 24 hours in the 1905 London to Edinburgh trial. Soon extra wheels were added to make, first, tricycles, and then cars that had an equally good reputation. One Lagonda car called the Torpedo took Gunn to first place in the extremely arduous Moscow to St Petersburg trial in 1910. Czar Nicholas II was much impressed and 'greatly favoured' Lagondas as a result. It was largely Russian orders that kept Lagonda going until Gunn, who put his heart and soul into everything he did, died from overwork in 1920.

The firm was then reorganised along military lines by Brigadier-General Francis Metcalfe to provide handsome rivals to W. O. Bentley's 3-litre cars. Metcalfe kept a stiff upper lip during the desperate days of the Depression that swept away their sporting opponent. As an honourable man, Metcalfe included provisions for Lagonda going into receivership when a syndicate of amateur racing drivers appealed to him to produce a 4.5-litre version of his 3-litre car, just as Bentley had done before.

The resulting Lagonda M45, so called because it had a 4.5-litre engine by the independent manufacturer, Meadows, was no mean performer despite its great bulk, retaining the 3-litre's excellent handling and superb brakes. But its most remarkable feature was the extraordinary torque of its six-cylinder in-line engine that made it very easy to drive. All told it was a far better bargain than the costly new 3.5-litre Rolls-Bentley, especially when it was uprated to near

road-racing specification as the M45R, or Rapide.

Lagonda were dealt a bitter blow when Metcalfe, who had kept them going throughout the Depression, succumbed to cancer. Then the market for big sports cars in Britain collapsed for a while in 1935 when driving tests, pedestrian crossings and the 30mph speed limit were introduced almost simultaneously. The works at Staines filled up with unsold Rapides and a receiver was appointed to run down the operation.

But Lagonda had powerful friends, none better than solicitor Alan Good and former Bentley boys like Dr J. Dudley Benjafield, who moved to form a consortium to keep the firm alive. In fact, Benjafield and the Lagonda specialist garage Fox and Nicholls contrived to enter Rapides at Le Mans that year, with outstanding results: the Spanish-born English enthusiast Luis Fontes won in the Fox and Nicholls car against the fastest cars in the world from Bugatti, Alfa Romeo, Delahaye and Duesenberg. The way Benjafield challenged for second place before being slowed to 13th by gear trouble proved that the win was no mere fluke. Such good fortune would have been the making of many other firms, but the publicity was of little immediate help to Lagonda who were pronounced bankrupt the following day.

It did serve to convince W. O. Bentley, however, that an approach to Good was worthwhile. He managed to escape the shackles of Rolls-Royce, who had bought his name and services along with his firm four years earlier, declaring his support for Good on that fateful day. With the win at Le Mans and the prospect of W. O. Bentley as chief designer, Good was able to raise enough money to take over Lagonda. His avowed intention was to take the national title of 'Best Car in the World' away from Rolls-Royce. Good pursued this ideal with a one-model policy: diversification into too many variants had been the real cause of Lagonda's earlier troubles. Bentley set to work on the design of the model that they hoped would capture that coveted title.

Initially, the old Meadows engine was uprated into Sanctions 1, 2 and 3 form – so called because its original manufacturer, Harry Meadows, sanctioned the changes – with stylist Frank Feeley producing outstanding bodies. In their ultimate form, these Lagondas were known as LG45, for Lagonda-Good. But they were intended only as interim models on the way to a virtually identical car powered by a new 4.5-litre V12 engine that Bentley was designing. By the time it appeared towards the end of 1938, war was on the way. It is one of the ironies of life that it lacked the torque that made the straight-six such an exceptional machine. The V12 may not have been the very best Lagonda, but such is the glamour attached to having so many cylinders that it is the model with a singularly romantic appeal. And that to most people is what Lagondas are all about.

SPECIFICATION

Country of origin: Great Britain.

Manufacturer: Lagonda.

Model: V12.

Year: 1937.

Engine: V12 cylinder, overhead camshaft, 4480cc.

Transmission: 4 forward ratios, live rear axle.

Body: Open or closed, 2 or 4 seats.

Wheelbase: 132in (3353mm).

Length: 206in (5232mm).

Height: 68in (1727mm).

Width: 72in (1829mm).

Maximum speed: 107mph (172km/h).

9.0in × 1.5in
(228 × 38mm)
cast iron drum brakes
front and rear

105mph (169km/h)
speedo was mounted
to the far left of the
dashboard. Maximum
speed was only 73mph
(117km/h)

Steering wheel could
be adjusted up and down
and forwards and backwards

M.G. TC MIDGET

4-cylinder in-line engine,
1250cc 54.4 bhp at 5200 rpm;
twin SU carburettors

Spindly 19in (482mm)
'knock-off' wire wheels
had a section of only
4.5in (114mm)

Rear 'slab' fuel
tank – capacity
13.5 gallons
(61 litres)

M.G. TC MIDGET

I T IS HARD to imagine anything more quaintly English than the early perpendicular M.G. At the time the first examples were conceived in 1922, as special-bodied versions of the mundane Morris Cowley, such lines were fashionable. Their creator was Cecil Kimber, who ran Morris Motors' main agents, Morris Garages, in Oxford: hence the name M.G. The demand for these rather exclusive cars – which were more profitable than the normal range – was so great that Kimber was able to expand into a new factory at Abingdon in 1930. Sales were also stimulated by ringing the changes on basic Morris mechanical components to give the M.Gs more sporting performance.

During the five years which followed, almost everything changed except the car's appearance. Kimber had long been obsessed with motifs like octagons, and these eight-sided circles appeared in every conceivable spot on his cars. They not only framed the car's name to make up the company badge, but encircled the instruments, and were even cast into structures such as the scuttle, under the skin. In this form they only came to light when the body was taken off for a major overhaul.

Even more effort went into improving the mechanical specification, fuelled by an intense involvement with racing and record-breaking that covered the marque in glory between 1930 and 1935. The chief competition came from cars made by Austin, Morris's great rival in the mass market. Such was the determination of Kimber and his team at Abingdon to produce the best sports cars in the world that they disregarded their profit margins, spending far more on development than the firm's owner Lord Nuffield

– formerly William Morris – deemed advisable. As a result, he curtailed all competition activities in 1935 and ordered M.G. to design new models using only the cheap mass-produced mechanical parts made for other cars produced by the Nuffield Group.

In retrospect, we can see that Morris was right. With an all-time-high figure of two million unemployed and with Britain only just emerging from six years of economic depression, Abingdon needed to make plenty of cheap, reliable cars, not just a handful of exotic little racers which had become so highly tuned that they were too daunting for the average buyer. Abingdon was horrified at having to give up racing, but jobs were scarce so the racing men buckled down to making what Nuffield wanted.

By far the biggest seller had been the small M.G. Midget, because it was their cheapest model. So they returned to their original concept for the 1929 Midget and raided Nuffield parts bins for whatever could be used to give it a similar performance to the far faster 1935 Midget. The simplest solution was to give the new car a bigger engine, a cheap 1292cc slogger rather than the more advanced, but no more powerful, 939cc unit. Kimber was allowed full rein over the body, however, and, to a certain extent, the chassis, so the new M.G. not only looked like a 'proper one' – functional, with octagons for embellishment – but it handled like one: 'Safety Fast', to use Abingdon's famous slogan.

When the first of these new models, the TA, was shown in 1936, M.G. enthusiasts howled in rage at the loss of their racing engines, replaced by the uninspiring heart of a boring Morris saloon car. But,

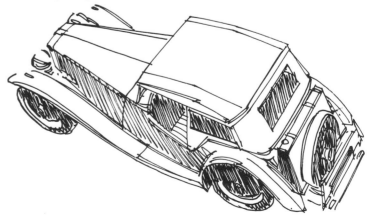

to their amazement, the new Midget could be made to perform better in the hands of the average motorist because it was easier to drive. It sold well until it was replaced by the TB in 1939. The new model looked almost exactly the same, but had a stronger and more modern 1250cc engine which had been developed for Morris's latest saloon. Happily, this unit was uncommonly amenable to tuning for higher performance, which pleased the more fanatical sporting motorist. Already a philosophy was emerging that almost anything under the skin of an M.G. could be changed, just so long as it still looked and drove like one.

The next five years at Abingdon were spent building tanks and parts for aircraft as M.G Midgets endeared themselves to servicemen, such as RAF pilots, because they could be as exciting to drive as planes were to fly, and were still quite economical to run on war-time petrol rations.

When the war was over, the priority was to produce as much as quickly as possible, for a market starved of new cars, rather than to waste time perfecting a new design. Abingdon was able to put the M.G. Midget back into production as early as November 1945 with only minimal modifications as the TC.

The cost of winning the war had nearly crippled Britain economically, so much so that exports took priority over everything. In fact, the only way to get steel to build new cars was for a manufacturer to be able to prove that it had a substantial export market. The results as Abingdon hit the export trail were extraordinary. From exporting 15 per cent of their annual product before the war, they found they could now sell 60 per cent, partly because the Midget epitomised an era of flying jackets, fun and fighting, and partly because it was the first car off the mark into the great untapped American market.

The Americans loved its 'wobbly' wire wheels and solid front axle. As U.S. servicemen went home, they were inclined to take a TC almost as a spoil of war. It showed that they had been 'where the action was'. An M.G. Midget could not have been more different from the cars favoured by the folks who had stayed at home. The low-slung chassis, upright radiator, separate wings, cutaway doors, slab tank and exposed headlights reflected the glories of a bygone age. If a man was old enough to fight for his country, he was old enough to drive a real car, not a sloppy sedan.

It was cars like the M.G. TC that brought the good times back to the British motor industry. During those early years, M.Gs were in such demand that foreign car importers forced dealers to take two of the cheap German Volkswagens for every one M.G. The dealers then unloaded the Volkswagen Beetles at a discount, reaping in their profit from M.G. Midgets. These classic British sports cars not only helped to save their country from economic ruin, but re-established Germany's industry, too!

SPECIFICATION

Country of origin: Great Britain

Manufacturer: M.G.

Model: TC Midget.

Year: 1945.

Engine: 4-cylinder in-line, overhead valve, 1250cc.

Transmission: 4 forward ratios, live rear axle.

Body: Open, 2 seats.

Wheelbase: 94in (2388mm).

Length: 140in (3543mm).

Height: 53in (1346mm).

Width: 56in (1422mm).

Maximum speed: 75mph (121km/h).

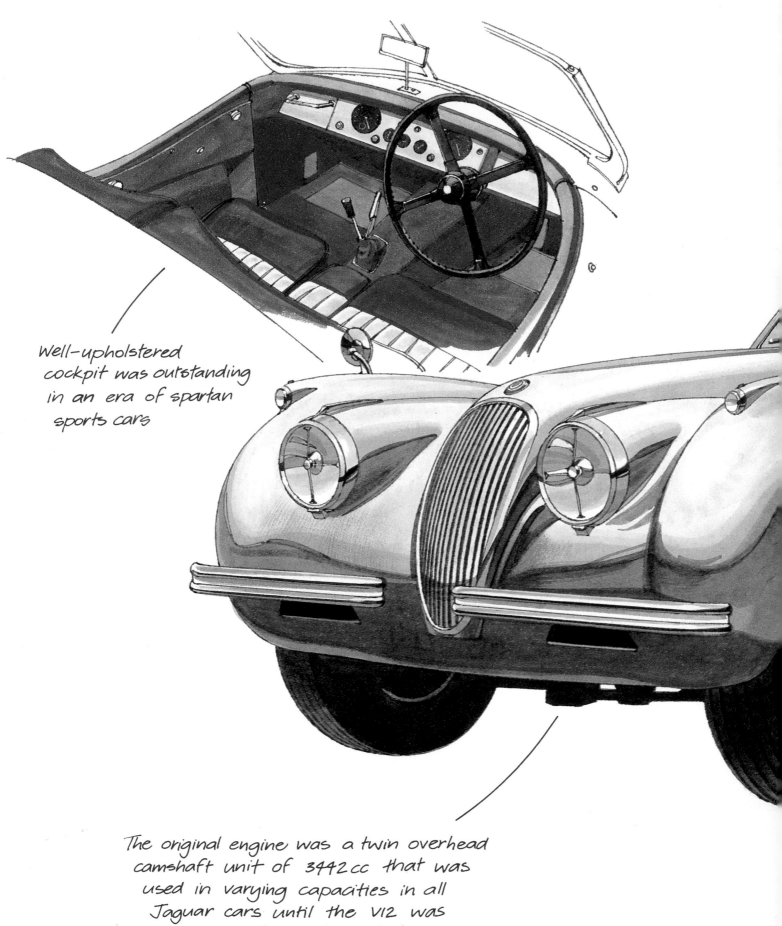

Well-upholstered
cockpit was outstanding
in an era of spartan
sports cars

The original engine was a twin overhead
camshaft unit of 3442cc that was
used in varying capacities in all
Jaguar cars until the V12 was
introduced for top models in 1971

JAGUAR XK120

Introduced at the
London Motor Show in 1948,
the styling was a complete
break with British tradition
and an instant success

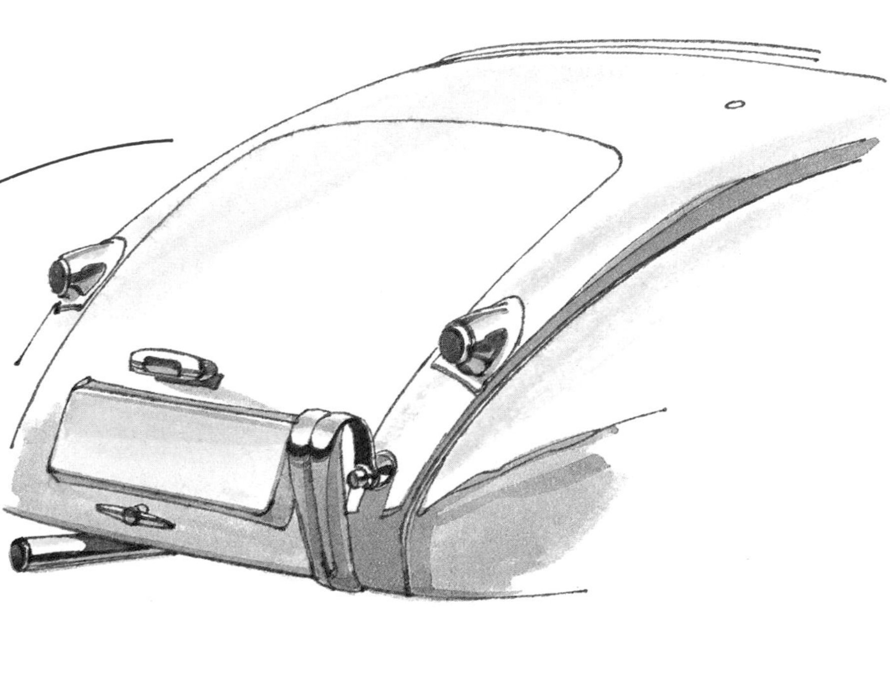

Body was a true
roadster – the hood
was fully detached
and stored in
the boot

JAGUAR XK120

THE JAGUAR XK120 was significant not only because it had one of the most beautiful bodies ever to grace a sporting car, but also because it had one of the most beautiful engines. There are many other reasons why the XK120 was a truly great car, but these were its most outstanding features. What is even more remarkable is that this wonderful car was produced almost by accident!

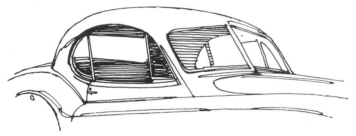

The engine, which looked more like a sculpture in cast iron topped off with elegant polished aluminium than anything mechanical, was the world's first twin overhead camshaft hemispherical-headed power unit to be put into normal production. Such exotic creations had previously been the province of only the rarest and most advanced racing cars and planes.

It was designed during wartime firewatching sessions by Jaguar's charismatic leader William Lyons, with his chief engineer, Bill Heynes, engine specialist Claude Baily and development ace Walter Hassan, who had been responsible for running the racing Bentleys throughout their greatest years. They drew up this engine in the long hours after their normal work, while watching for enemy air attacks on the Jaguar factory in Coventry.

After the Second World War, Jaguar – like M.G. – produced cars that were simply updated versions of pre-war models, while the Famous Four set about designing a new machine that was worthy of this magnificent engine. Lyons had decided that this should be a saloon car, because such models were the mainstay of Jaguar production. Heynes, meantime, revised the pre-war chassis with independent front suspension to make it thoroughly competitive against what was expected to be a whole new breed of rival cars. This chassis was then introduced for existing saloons, which retained for the time being pre-war-type bodies and traditional pushrod engines.

The new suspension system took its inspiration from Citroën's revolutionary Traction Avant of 1934, the 'Maigret' car. The wishbone and torsion bar design saved space and made a vast improvement to the car's ride and handling, when used in conjunction with the stiff new chassis, introduced on the Jaguar Mark V saloon in 1948.

Unfortunately the new engine, codenamed XK, could not be produced immediately in sufficient quantities for the saloon cars, because it meant setting up a new line of machine tools. These were not only very expensive, but also in short supply. However, the engine could be made in small numbers on existing machinery, so Lyons decided to build a few sports cars as publicity for the firm and the engine.

Heynes and Hassan shortened the new chassis for this exercise while Lyons designed a body which could be made by just a few skilled panelbeaters. The team did not anticipate sufficient demand for the sports car to have to make provision for its body panels to be stamped out in large quantities on huge presses.

As a result, Lyons felt few constraints while dictating its lines. Fairly complex panels could be made relatively cheaply by hand, provided the few skilled workers that were available had sufficient time. Lyons took fullest advantage of this freedom to produce an extraordinarily beautiful new Jaguar, called the XK after its engine.

Initially it appeared necessary to market two versions of the engine, in four-cylinder and six-cylinder forms. The economy version was intended for Britain, which was still suffering petrol rationing, and the more powerful six-cylinder for the rest of the world. Naturally the first sports model, designed to appeal to the export market, had the more glamorous six-cylinder 160bhp engine when the car was unveiled in October 1948. The four-cylinder XK waited in the wings.

The reception for the Jaguar XK120, so called because it would reach speeds of at least 120mph (192km/h), took everybody at Jaguar by surprise. They had been so obsessed with the dramatic new saloon intended to take the engine that they did not realise the sales potential of a sports car. Part of the attraction was that Lyons's asking price was only £998 – or $4000 at the time – in line with his previous policy of keeping the small-scale production sports cars in the same price range as the saloons.

The XK120 was such a bargain that many people did not believe it was capable of the extraordinary performance that Jaguar claimed. So, with the odd modification such as an aero screen, which was acceptable at that time, Jaguar sent an early version to the nearest motorway at Jabbeke, Belgium. Assembled journalists watched as test driver 'Soapy' Sutton – a character straight out of Biggles – returned a speed of no less than 132.6mph (212km/h) on an officially timed run. After that amazing demonstration, demand for the new car was overwhelming and the company immediately dropped all idea of producing a four-cylinder economy XK and had to make plans for a mass-produced body.

Many other manufacturers were waiting in line, like Jaguar, for new bodies because models with pre war styling were beginning to look very old-fashioned. They could not afford to make the fashionable new all-enveloping bodies themselves because the vital machine tools were so expensive, which meant that they had to wait until independent bodymakers had sufficient capacity. As a result the first 250 XK120s produced in 1949 and 1950 had bodies beaten by hand from aluminium because it was easier to work and more readily available than steel.

This had the happy effect of making these cars lighter than average and even better suited to competition. Six of the earliest XK120s were given to well-known competition drivers as part of the original publicity campaign. One of the six was Lyons's son-in-law, Ian Appleyard, who proceeded to win the Alpine Rally in three consecutive years from 1950 to 1952 and the Tulip Rally in 1951. Another lightweight XK120 finished as high as third at Le Mans in 1950 before Jaguar produced special racing versions to win the great event.

Suddenly all the world wanted an XK, or the big new Mark VII saloon powered by the XK engine. Both cars followed M.G.'s export trail to America, and in their wake came a beautiful fixed-head coupé version of the XK120 in 1951, that was reminiscent of Bugatti's pre-war masterpiece, the Atlantic. The range was completed by a drop-head coupé combining the roadster's open appeal with the saloon-like comforts of the fixed head.

SPECIFICATION

Country of origin: Great Britain.

Manufacturer: Jaguar.

Model: XK120.

Year: 1948.

Engine: 6-cylinder in-line, twin overhead camshaft, 3442cc.

Transmission: 4 forward ratios, live rear axle.

Body: Open, 2 seats.

Wheelbase: 102in (2591mm).

Length: 174in (4420mm).

Height: 153in (4636mm) hood erect.

Width: 62in (1562mm).

Maximum speed: 125mph (201km/h).

Called a 'Barchetta' (little boat). The body was designed by Carrozzeria Touring of Milan as one of their first all-enveloping sports car designs

Neat, tidy and functional rear-end treatment of this tiny (149in/3785mm long) bombshell

FERRARI 212 BARCHETTA

V12 engine was designed by
Gioacchino Colombo to a
specification by Enzo Ferrari
that he simply wanted
something that
'sounded like a 12'

FERRARI 212 BARCHETTA

THE CARS MADE by the doyen of grand prix racing, Enzo Ferrari, have always been built around their engines, with the power plant taking precedence over all other aspects of design. The early Ferraris were built primarily for competition, but in an era when such cars could also be driven on the road. As the demands of racing became ever more specialised, later Ferraris had to be one thing or the other, either racing cars, or road cars.

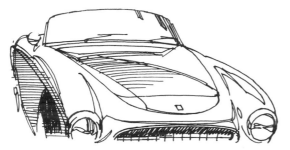

Although the chassis, suspension and brakes were reasonably advanced when the first cars were built in 1947, the design stagnated after that as Ferrari's efforts were concentrated on ever more powerful engines. It was not until the 1960s that these aspects were brought up to date, making great classics of the earlier cars because they were so far ahead of their contemporary rivals. Bodywork has also varied from the beautiful to the bizarre, with the first barchettas – or little boats – as the greatest classics because they had the best combination of body, mechanics and chassis.

Enzo Ferrari, a metalworker's son born in Modena, northern Italy, in 1898, became a works driver for Alfa Romeo in the 1920s before running their racing team under his own banner, Scuderia Ferrari, from 1929. It was at this point that he adopted as his insignia the *cavallino rampante,* or prancing horse, which was retained when he started building his own cars. There are varying tales concerning his adoption of this distinctive logo, but the most likely is that it was the emblem of the air force squadron in which his brother died during the First World War.

From the very beginning, Ferrari was a 'concept man', laying down the general lines of how a car, and especially its engine, should be designed, and then leaving the detail work to others. When he started his own firm in Modena in 1946, he was a fervent admirer of the V12-cylinder power units used in Packard and Delage cars and he commissioned former Alfa Romeo engineer Gioacchino Colombo to produce an engine with 'the song of a twelve'.

Ferrari's briefs, based purely on instinctive ideas, were often as sketchy as that, but he knew what he wanted and the sound of his V12s has never been surpassed. The theory behind the use of 12 cylinders was as good as the sound they made, providing a reasonable balance between maximum power and minimum complexity. Colombo's design was not perfect, but it was much improved by Ferrari's lifelong associate, Luigi Bazzi, an exceptionally gifted development engineer who had been part of the team at Alfa Romeo.

Colombo's V12, built to a classical 60-degree formation with alloy cylinder castings, single overhead camshafts, and a crankshaft turned from a single billet of steel, established the characteristics which made Ferrari engines famous. Not only did it sound like a real racing engine, but it smelled like one, with the distinctive tang of burning oil pouring from its exhaust pipes. The fumes were the result of

very generous lubrication for the highly stressed valvegear. The valves ran in bronze guides that matched the expansion rate of the alloy castings better than steel, but wore quickly. As a race progressed, this deficiency allowed oil to pass into the combustion chambers, where it burned especially well with the very rich mixture provided by a multitude of Weber carburettors. Thus, the harder the engine was revved the better it went.

It certainly encouraged such use, being endowed with an almost animal-like response that racing drivers loved, although it took an exceptionally talented one to use such a fierce unit to best advantage. Inferior drivers simply over-revved it, but because the lubrication was so good they got away with it. This meant that the early Ferraris could be driven virtually into the ground, then recover to grind on, wreathed in smoke, to defeat lesser racing cars.

The first Colombo-engined Type 166 Ferraris had 1.5-litre engines and a chassis made from two strong tubes, cross-braced, and carrying simple transverse leaf independent front suspension, their live rear axle being suspended by half-elliptic springs. Like the engine, the gearbox was fairly advanced, having five forward ratios to cope with the ferocious power output. But the traditional worm and peg steering left a lot to be desired. Enzo Ferrari treated it as the devil he knew, refusing to opt for a better design until it had been proved totally inadequate. The fact that the steering was eventually improved almost beyond recognition and that the Colombo engine was simultaneously bored out to 2.5 litres made the new Type 212 a much better car.

The earliest Ferraris were ugly cars, featuring a square-lined body behind a gaping grille which harmonised with nothing in particular. They were called Spyder Corsas, meaning racing carriages, running with exposed wire wheels as pure racing cars and with cycle-type wings in events for sports cars. As such, they provided a brutal but effective means of winning for the lucky few who drove them.

But it was obvious that the bodywork needed improvement, especially as the vestigial cycle-type wings were about to be outlawed for international sports car racing. Organisers had decided that sports cars ought to look like sports cars, rather than thinly disguised grand prix cars, so that they could provide an alternative attraction. In common with many racing car builders, Ferrari did not make its own bodies at that time, leaving that task to specialists. As a result, considerable competition developed between coachbuilders to establish who could make the best bodies for such rapid and influential machines.

The prize fell to the Italian firm of Touring, who produced the first barchetta body on a Type 212 chassis in 1950 before the model went into limited production the following year. Although a wide grille had to be retained to provide Colombo's engine with adequate cooling, it now blended into the taut and sinuous lines of the body so well that it became the classic post-war sports car shape.

Imitation is the sincerest form of flattery and the body and chassis were copied by a variety of builders, including John Tojeiro in Britain, who subsequently sold his design to A.C. for their Ace sports car. This classic conception was then uprated with an American V8 engine in 1962 for the A.C. Cobra and lives on in all manner of replicas still sold to enthusiasts seeking the ultimate sports car.

SPECIFICATION

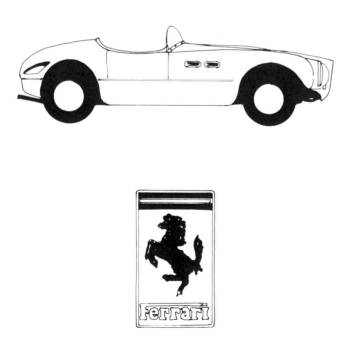

Country of origin: Italy.

Manufacturer: Ferrari.

Model: 212 barchetta.

Year: 1951.

Engine: V12 cylinder, overhead camshaft, 2562cc.

Transmission: 5 forward ratios, live rear axle.

Body: Open, 2 seats.

Wheelbase: 87in (2250mm).

Length: 149in (3785mm).

Height: 46in (1168mm).

Width: 62in (1575mm).

Maximum speed: 130mph (209km/h).

Dummy radiator shell
of later production
Continentals

4566cc engine produced speeds of 50, 80
and 100mph (80, 128 and 160 km/h)
in the intermediate gears

BENTLEY CONTINENTAL

The most beautiful Bentley of all — body styled by
J.P. Blatchley, with performance to match.
In 1951 the prototype (affectionately known
as Olga) lapped the Monthléry track
at 120mph (193 km/h)

THE BENTLEY CONTINENTAL in its R-type form was an instant classic, because it was not only the world's fastest saloon of its time, but also one of the most attractive and refined cars ever built. Like so many great machines, it owed its existence to one man, known only as H. I. F. Evernden, chief project engineer at Rolls-Royce. He pushed the car through its gestation period almost against the wishes of a rather reactionary management.

Evernden's achievement, in company with the Rolls-Royce Motor Car Division's chief stylist, J. P. Blatchley, was made all the more remarkable by the restrictions under which they worked. Both men were convinced there was a market for a high-performance lightweight saloon using standard components, and were allowed to follow up their ideas only because they had previously toed a conservative company line. But even when they were at last allowed free creativity they were kept on a short rein and permitted to change few aspects of the staid R-type Bentley which was to form the basis for the Continental. Fortunately they were given more scope with the body – although it was decreed that it still had to look like the 'real Bentley', retaining the traditional massive radiator.

Evernden sold the project to the management on the premise that he could produce a car which 'not only looked beautiful, but possessed a high maximum speed coupled with a correspondingly high rate of acceleration, together with excellent handling qualities and roadability.' They gave way grudgingly to his quiet insistence only because of increasing criticism of their adoption for Bentley of the slogan 'The Silent Sports Car'. Many people pointed out that although Bentleys built at Crewe since 1931 were

silent, they were certainly not sports cars like those built by W. O. Bentley at Cricklewood. They were, in reality, Rolls-Royces with a different radiator grille and badges.

The ample 120in (3050mm) wheelbase and the 58.5in (1486mm) track of the standard Rolls-Royce-inspired Bentley saloon had to be retained, but Evernden was allowed to uprate the normal 4.5-litre six-cylinder engine providing he did not encroach on the refinement and flexibility of which Rolls-Royce were so proud. In the stolid traditional way, they would not reveal how much power and torque he extracted, merely explaining that it was 'sufficient' . . . for a target of no less than 120mph (192km/h), or two miles (3.2km) per minute. Evernden calculated that this could be achieved if the weight of the car was reduced from 4100 to 3640lb (1860 to 1650kg) and the gear ratios altered to allow a standard four-speed gearbox to run on a direct-drive top rather than an overdrive.

Aerodynamics had only limited influence on Evernden's equations, since the management decreed that this brave new car should retain the Bentley grille of old. But after a lot of detailed and diplomatic persuasion, Evernden managed to get the height of this imposing edifice reduced by 1.5in (38mm) – 'and no further', said the management, thinking already that they might have to kill off the project to preserve the company's dignified image. The enforced bluff front was partly compensated, however, by Blatchley's remarkable styling, which made use of a wind tunnel to perfect an almost feline tail, now known as a fastback.

The rest was achieved through fanatical attention to detail by the London coachbuilders Mulliner, who panelled the entire body in aluminium rather than Bentley's standard steel. Even the bumpers and seat frames were fashioned in alloy. Finally, as the Rolls management wavered on whether or not to put this beautiful car into production, Evernden persuaded them to allow an inch to be pared from the prototype's rather high roofline so that the magic speed of 120mph (192km/h) could be achieved. He received solid backing from Bentley's Paris agent, Walter Sleator, who had been responsible for a prototype of similar conception before the war. Sleater was convinced that the car would sell itself to his clients, who had the advantage of miles of fast open road that were not to be found in Britain at the time. And so this marvellous new Bentley was named the Continental.

Of the 208 models built between 1952 and 1958, 193 had Mulliner's special body, with the balance shared between various different coachbuilders, who had to agree not to exceed a similar target weight. Customers were also warned that any extras – other than a radio – would increase the weight enough to reduce the Continental's fine performance. They also had to sign an agreement not to race their new car: such activities were beneath the dignity of anything associated with Rolls-Royce, even when the car was called a Bentley.

True to his word, Sleator became the biggest importer, selling 32 Continentals in France at a high premium, with 28 going to America, 100 to wealthy English customers anxious to lose no time on the run down to the South of France, and the rest being scattered throughout the world.

To drive a Bentley Continental in the 1950s was to move into a different world. The reduction in weight made so much difference to its handling and acceleration, but even more significant was the fact that Mulliner's bodies were so beautifully built that the Continental's silent cruising ability was to remain unequalled for more than a decade.

Production was divided into five differently lettered series, from A to E. In practice there was little difference between an A and a B series, the C-type was an interim model with the option of automatic transmission on the way to the near-identical D and E with an enlarged 3.75in (95.25mm) bore engine giving 4.9-litres and an even more relaxed run up to 120mph (192km/h). Left-hand-drive cars using manual gearboxes normally had an excellent steering column change, whereas the right-hand-drive manual Continentals felt more like the Bentleys of old with their precise right-hand gear levers.

More than any of its contemporaries, the Bentley Continental – with its supreme combination of speed, silence, smoothness, dignity and restrained use of first-class materials fashioned by top craftsmen – could aspire to share the title of the 'Best Car in the World', with Rolls-Royce.

SPECIFICATION

Country of origin: Great Britain.

Manufacturer: Bentley.

Model: Continental.

Year: 1952.

Engine: 6-cylinder in-line, overhead inlet side exhaust, 4566cc.

Transmission: 4 forward ratios, live rear axle.

Body: Fixed-head coupé, 4 seats.

Wheelbase: 120in (2540mm).

Length: 207in (5245mm).

Height: 65in (1651mm).

Width: 72in (1816mm).

Maximum speed: 117mph (188km/h).

1954 Eldorado found favour with
buyers and 2150 were sold, a
four-fold increase over the '53 model!
Note the metal tonneau cover

Ribbed bright metal
panels on rear fenders

Massive tail fins
and lavish chrome
characterised these
cars

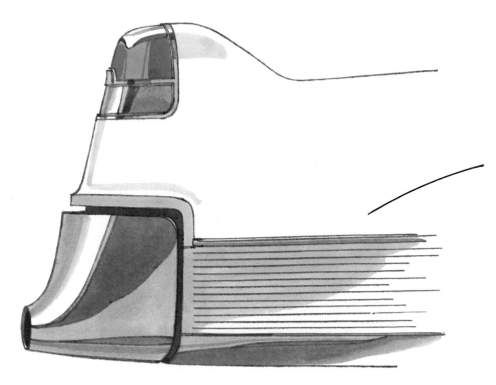

CADILLAC ELDORADO

331 cu in overhead valve V8 engine generating 230 bhp

Gold Cadillac crest on doors

CADILLAC ELDORADO

IT IS DOUBTFUL whether anybody will ever produce a more flamboyant car for general sale than the first Cadillac Eldorado. Some even had chromium-plated brake pedals until it dawned on their manufacturer that they might become too slippery. But owning an Eldorado was a clear demonstration that you had 'arrived'.

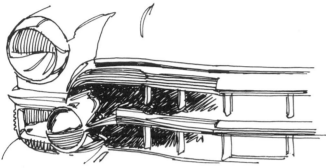

The Eldorado represented part of General Motors' response to critics who said that post-war American sedans and convertibles were boring. At first, such opinions counted for little in the corporate mind. Americans were rushing out to buy anything new, especially cars, after the years of limited choice and supply during the war. Then the General's minions noticed that a lot of people were happy to pay extra for 'sporty' cars such as the M.G. TC and Jaguar XK120

By 1953, such trends could no longer be dismissed as freaks of fashion. So the General attacked the problem on two fronts, by introducing its own sports car, the Chevrolet Corvette, and the car they thought would be irresistible to their customers: the Cadillac Eldorado.

If ever a car could symbolise Hollywood's golden years, it was this model. Cadillac had a head start on their chief rivals, Packard, because they had broken away from the traditional vertical radiator grille back in 1941. As Packard tried in vain to adapt their proud edifice to modern styling, Cadillac were able to snatch the laurels by introducing, simultaneously, an egg-crate grille, an upright simulated air scoop on each rear wing, and prominent fins for the tail. As Americans were presented with more choice in the early 1950s Cadillacs featured ever larger and more ornate grilles, scoops and fins. Such ostentatious

demonstrations of affluence were supplemented by chromium-plated eyebrows for the headlights, enormous bumpers and even bigger over-riders. These were raised so high and projected so far they were named after the prominent charms of a TV hostess called Dagmar. No wonder the kids hanging around the jukebox, including a laundry van driver named Elvis Presley, called it the dreamboat.

Nothing else glittered quite like an Eldorado. It was America's most expensive car and cost almost twice as much as the regular Series 62 Cadillac convertible on which it was based. It also made a small fortune for the secretary who won the in-house competition to find a name for the new car. She suggested that it should be called Eldorado – Spanish for 'the golden one' – because Eldorado was the lost land of the South American Incas, abounding in gold, gems and works of art.

The Eldorado was an artistic triumph for Harley Earl, who had led the General Motors' 1941 styling revolution which established post-war shapes and features. Its ancestry could be traced to the experimental cars he designed for Buick, one of Cadillac's partners in General Motors. These machines of the late 1940s, the XP-8 and XP-9, became the Buick Le Sabre and XP-300 of the 1950s.

One of the Buicks' chief styling features was a 'panoramic' windscreen, which duly appeared on the Cadillac. In fact, Earl felt so strongly about this wraparound windshield that the Eldorado's body was designed around it. The doors and rear quarters of regular Series 62 convertibles were cut away to form a gently angled notch above the rear wing's vertical 'scoop'. The intention was to emphasise the lines of the screen and its attendant wind deflectors.

The suspension was then lowered an inch to make the completed car look extra sleek and low at three or four inches (75-100mm) less than the overall height of a normal Series 62, with its old-fashioned windscreen.

A special hood in a new man-made fabric called Orlon disappeared into a well behind the seats, to be covered, if the driver had the time and patience, by trim panels. In brief, it was necessary to first extract the cover, made in three pieces from the new glass fibre which was being used for the Corvette's body. This was not easy, as the lengthy mouldings were contained in a vinyl plastic pouch strapped to the luggage boot floor at the bottom of the well. Yards of hood material then had to be folded neatly into place and dropped into the well, with the roots remaining in place around the body's rim. The glass fibre side panels were clamped in place with snap fasteners and further vinyl flaps. It then needed two people to manoeuvre the centre section into place so that it could be secured by chrome locking pins. In the event of a sudden downpour, it was impossible to reverse the process without at least two people to do it and a soaking for the occupants. It would be some time before power-operated hoods became a reality on the Great American Convertible.

There were many other special features to the Eldorado including simulated leather plastic grips on the steering wheel, 'for safety', allied with a chromium-plated horn push with a point as big as a Dagmar which enraged a young lawyer called Ralph Nader. In later years, he was quick to point out that if the driver had an accident and escaped being impaled on the horn push he could still crack his skull on the sturdy chromium-plated liners which surrounded another 'safety feature' – a dashboard crashpad made from softly padded leather-grained plastic. Lashings of potentially dangerous chromium-plated metal which distinguished other aspects of the interior included trimming on the doors and arm rests, and a massive central ashtray.

In keeping with its exclusive nature, the Eldorado was available only in four colours: Aztec Red, Azure Blue, Alpine White and Artisan Ochre, with red, blue or black and white for the interior. Thus it was possible to order a yellow car with blue or red trimming. Whitewall tyres were standard, along with a radio and windscreen washers. General Motors considered the Eldorado so exclusive that its name did not appear anywhere on the exterior, only on a gold crest above the instrument panel and in decorative script on the kickplates. If anybody remained in doubt that the Eldorado was an aristocratic car they only had to refer to those who rode in them: the best examples being Dwight Eisenhower and his wife, Mamie, symbolic of all that was good in America, on their way to the White House in 1953.

SPECIFICATION

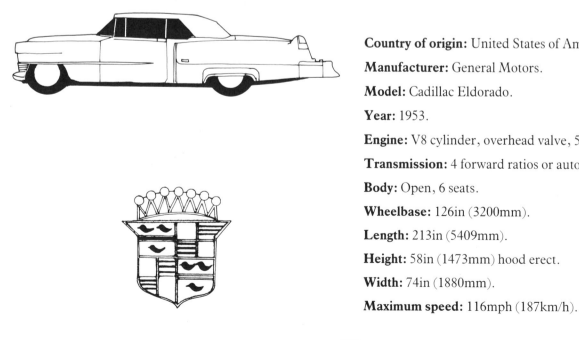

Country of origin: United States of America.

Manufacturer: General Motors.

Model: Cadillac Eldorado.

Year: 1953.

Engine: V8 cylinder, overhead valve, 5414cc.

Transmission: 4 forward ratios or automatic.

Body: Open, 6 seats.

Wheelbase: 126in (3200mm).

Length: 213in (5409mm).

Height: 58in (1473mm) hood erect.

Width: 74in (1880mm).

Maximum speed: 116mph (187km/h).

Clutch and gearbox were mounted at the rear of the car, in unit with the final drive

Downdraught Weber carburettor

Aurelia engine was a 60 V6, with overhead valves, developing 118bhp at 5000rpm

LANCIA AURELIA 2500GT

Aurelia was the concept of Gianni Lancia and was
the first true GT production car. Its 2451cc
engine gave 115mph (185km/h) — excellent
for its day

THE LANCIA AURELIA in its B20 form will always be remembered as the world's first GT, or grand touring car on the way to its high point in the 2500GT. But it was even more distinguished than that: it had the first production V6 engine, and semi-trailing arm – independent rear suspension which set a continuing trend, especially when linked with a transaxle combining the gearbox and rear axle for ultimate balance. As if this were not enough, the Aurelia was one of the first cars to use radial-ply tyres and so improve its handling even further. Such technical innovation was only to be expected of the great Italian car maker in the 1950s. Twenty years earlier Lancia had pioneered unitary construction, in which the body and chassis are combined for maximum rigidity and strength, and there had been a host of inventions in between.

Most of these inventions sprang from the fertile brain of Vincenzo Lancia, who inspired other engineers to perfect his ideas while his mind strayed along even more radical paths. As the story goes, the first vision came to Vincenzo when he was caught in a storm while sailing on Lake Como, near his factory in Turin. Great waves battered the bows of his boat, but Vincenzo did not panic – he just pondered on how much stronger the steel hull was than the chassis of the cars he made.

His thoughts on the subject spanned five years until one day in March 1921 he called his engineers together and told them he wanted to build a car with a hull like that of a ship. They confirmed his worst fears that a machine of such rigidity would be unmanageable using the stiff springs and beam axles much favoured at the time. The front wheels would be worst affected as they bounced from rut to rut with no whipping chassis to provide more supple spring-

ing. They also had to steer the car, which made it essential they stayed in contact with the ground for as long as possible. Such problems had been overcome on motor cycles, however, where a rigid frame was essential. So Lancia chose an independent front suspension system using the sliding pillars which had been adopted on the British Morgan from motor cycle practice.

Once the suspension problem was solved, Lancia authorised development of the rest of the car, which, by coincidence, had a V4 engine like that used in steam boats, where the weight was concentrated low in the bottom of the hull with the cylinder banks following its contours. The chief attraction to Lancia was that such an engine was shorter than a conventional in-line unit, leaving more room for passengers. Thus was born Lancia's first great car, the Lambda.

Still his mind wandered, not just on specific problems, but on cars as a whole. Lancia was fascinated by the study of aerodynamics, then in its infancy. He saw little difference between the way a car ploughed through the air and a ship through the water, so once more he turned to nautical practice. He swung the hull upside down for his next great car, the beautifully streamlined Aprilia saloon, the outstanding features of which were patented in April 1934.

Old Vincenzo died in 1937, but Lancia had by then taken on Vittorio Jano, possibly the greatest of all Italian motor engineers, who had been pensioned off by Alfa Romeo. It was Jano, and his brilliant assistant, Francesco de Virgilio, who created the next great Lancia, the Aurelia. Its advanced specification had been dictated by the desire of Vincenzo's son, Gianni, to produce a car worthy of his father's name. As early as 1943 he decided it should be more comfortable than the rather cramped pre-war models,

but that it should sacrifice none of their nimble handling. This meant that it had to be roomier inside without growing larger outside. A six-cylinder engine was needed to provide the performance lost to an inevitably weightier body. The obvious problem was where to put the extra two cylinders without encroaching too far into the cabin.

It was then remembered that old Vincenzo had experimented with a V6 engine when he had had the same ideas about the Lambda 20 years earlier. The project had been abandoned because, like everybody else, he did not have engineers who could make an inherently out-of-balance engine run smoothly. But de Virgilio could, his triumph being demonstrated in 1947 with a modified Aprilia saloon. This little car's independent rear suspension was improved at the same time to put it far ahead of the rival swing axle system used by German cars in which one wheel was likely to tuck under with disastrous results for the handling even if the ride was better.

But still Gianni was not satisfied: his new car had to look more graceful as well as outperform its peers. So he called in Pinin Farina (the welding together of the names for Pininfarina came later) to work with Jano on a new body. This retained the Aprilia's pillarless construction, which meant that it was rather heavy when it had been made sufficiently rigid. Jano was therefore even more concerned to reduce unsprung weight and resorted to the transaxle he had designed for his last great Alfa Romeo, a 12-cylinder grand prix car of 1936.

The striking new Aurelia, codenamed B10, made its debut at the Turin Show in April 1950 and went on to perform well in rallies despite its weight and the fact that it was intended only as a luxurious new saloon. So the wheelbase was shortened and the 1.5-litre engine increased to 2 litres for the B20 fixed-head coupé – the world's first GT car – of 1951. Success followed success until de Virgilio extracted 118bhp from 2.5 litres in a low-line bodyshell for the 2500GT of 1953. Louis Chiron promptly celebrated by winning the Monte Carlo Rally.

Twenty versions of the Aurelia were made, ranging from long-wheelbase taxis to estate cars, with all sorts of special coachwork, before it was replaced by bigger, more luxurious cars. But already the Aurelia had led to the building of the D50, a grand prix car, before Ferrari took over the project complete with its creator, Jano. Much of the credit for the V6 Ferrari engines which followed was given to Enzo Ferrari's son Dino, but in reality they were largely the work of Jano. Once more he was pensioned off and shot himself in 1965 mistakenly believing he had an incurable disease. He did not live to see the V6 Dino engine take Lancia's Stratos supercar to glory in international rallies, sometimes challenged by Alfa Romeo's GTV that bore such a close resemblance to the long-gone Aurelia 2500GT.

SPECIFICATION

Country of origin: Italy.

Manufacturer: Lancia.

Model: Aurelia 2500GT.

Year: 1953.

Engine: Vee 6-cylinder, overhead valve, 2541cc.

Transmission: 4 forward ratios, transaxle.

Body: Fixed-head coupé, 2 seats.

Wheelbase: 104in (2642mm).

Length: 173in (4394mm).

Height: 54in (1359mm).

Width: 61in (1549mm).

Maximum speed: 115mph (185km/h).

Six-cylinder engine of 2996 cc was fed by a fuel injection system developed from that of the Messerschmitt BF109 fighter

Unique body was designed by Karl Wilfert; overall concept of the car was the work of Mercedes Benz chief engineer Rudolph Uhlenhaut. Car featured independent suspension all round and Alfin brake drums

MERCEDES-BENZ 300SL GULLWING

'Gullwing' doors, trademark of the 300SL, were necessary because abnormally deep sills were needed to cover the 300SL's space frame

Concealed retractable door handles

MERCEDES-BENZ 300SL GULLWING

WHEN MERCEDES PRODUCED their Gullwing coupé it was a vehicle not only of stunning appearance but of adventurous design. It was sadly flawed by a political decision which gave this marvellous machine a potentially lethal character.

The Gullwing sprang from Mercedes' need to re-establish their reputation for producing some of the world's fastest cars after their factories had been razed to the ground during the Second World War. Sports car racing offered the best opportunity for publicity when production returned to normal in the 1950s, so they took the already powerful six-cylinder engine of their 300S saloon as the major component of a new competition machine.

The move was made all the more attractive when they found that it could be tuned for even more power and ran well canted far to one side. This enabled a low bonnet line to be envisaged for streamlined bodywork which would compensate for the extreme power produced by pure racing units. In this way money would be saved on development and more made from the publicity success would bring to their normal cars. For the same reason, the production cars' suspension was retained, which is where the problems started.

It was impractical to modify a saloon car chassis sufficiently for competition, so designer Rudolph Uhlenhaut was given a free hand in that area. The chassis he produced became the world's finest real space frame, coming in ahead of that of the British genius, Colin Chapman with his Lotus Mark 6, by a matter of weeks. It was called a space frame because there was more space than frame in this elegant chassis, comprised of an intricate network of tubing

to locate essential items such as the engine, transmission, suspension and body. The network was stressed as beautifully as a spider's web, gaining strength as a result, and saving much of the weight wasted by conventional girders. It took hours of skilled welding to construct, but that didn't matter since Mercedes intended to produce only a few of these cars as a publicity exercise.

The same freedom was allowed when it came to the design of the body, which was not only extremely 'wind-cheating', but featured aircraft style gullwing doors so that the occupants could step down into the car over the high sides of the space frame. Lowering the tubing to ease entry would have compromised the frame's strength. Panelled in delicate aluminium, Mercedes' new car fully justified the title 300SL for three-litre Sport Leicht (German for light).

It was not the fastest sports racing car of its day because it used so many basic saloon car components, but it was so strong and reliable that the model won four of the five major events it contested in 1952. In company with the smaller Porsches, Mercedes could also claim to have the most dependable racing cars, which did their reputation no harm at all. They then withdrew from competition for a while to perfect new components hoping this would take them into the highest realms of sports car and grand prix racing, but it seemed a pity not to capitalise on the success of the Gullwing coupés.

So one was slightly remodelled as a road car to raise Mercedes' image even further at the New York Auto Show early in 1954. American dealers, led by European expatriate Max Hoffman, went wild, bombarding Mercedes with demands that they put this wonderful car into full-scale production. Mercedes knew this could never be feasible with a frame that took so long to produce by hand, but relented when they realised that if they produced the 300SL in small numbers at a very high price, people would flood into dealers' showrooms, just to look at it. And then, hopefully, some of them would buy Mercedes saloons. It was called creating showroom traffic.

And so the Gullwing went into production with the truly amazing quirk that the road cars were more powerful than the racers because Mercedes had learned, in the interim, how to replace carburettors with the fuel injection system from their aero engines!

The only trouble was that Mercedes' directors refused to allow Uhlenhaut to improve the rear suspension on grounds of cost. It was their time-honoured swing axle system that was cheap to produce and had provided an outstandingly comfortable ride on the rough pre-war roads. But now roads were improving, speeds were rising and the performance of cars increasing at the same time. This meant that the limitations of swing axle geometry, with its sudden loss of adhesion from wildly changing camber angles, were ever more glaringly exposed. And the more power you put through such a system, the more dangerous it became. Mercedes had been able to ignore this problem while the 300SL competition cars were being driven by highly skilled racing drivers; but now production versions were being released into the hands of ordinary drivers with 16 per cent more power and a top speed as high as 160mph (257km/h) when optional performance equipment was fitted!

It soon became evident that the only safe way to slow down suddenly in a Gullwing was when it was pointing straight ahead, otherwise you risked an almighty spin as the suspension flexed, with similar problems as one wheel tucked under when hurtling through a Z-bend. Even worse, if the Gullwing coupé overturned, there was a distinct possibility that the occupants might be trapped inside because they could not open the doors.

Fortunately, progress and the dictates of fashion soon caught up with the Gullwing. No sooner had the Americans got their Gullwings than they began clamouring for an open version. Mercedes eventually gave way and authorised Uhlenhaut to design the new chassis that such a car would need, as the high-sided cockpit – dictated by the old frame – could no longer be tolerated. Now that the frame had to be redesigned, there could be no objections on cost grounds to the incorporation of revised suspension mountings which would eliminate the worst effects of the swing axle geometry.

Uhlenhaut's arguments in favour of his new low-pivot suspension were made all the more convincing because it had now been incorporated in Mercedes saloons. And so the 300SL roadster of 1957 became a much more manageable car, helped in part because it was not as fast without the coupé's streamlined top. Nor as beautiful without those predatory Gullwing doors.

SPECIFICATION

Country of origin: West Germany.

Manufacturer: Daimler-Benz.

Model: Mercedes 300SL.

Year: 1954.

Engine: 6-cylinder in-line, overhead camshaft, 2996cc.

Transmission: 4 forward ratios, frame-mounted final drive.

Body: Fixed-head coupé, gullwing doors, 2 seats.

Wheelbase: 94in (2400mm).

Length: 180in (4572mm).

Height: 51in (1295mm).

Width: 70in (1778mm).

Maximum speed: 135mph (217km/h).

Engine was mounted
behind rear wheels (à la VW)
and during the production life
of the car it was developed for
ever increasing power output

PORSCHE 356 SPEEDSTER

The 356 Speedster was built chiefly as a loss leader for the American market

Body was first built in light alloy fixed-head form but after production was moved to Zuffenhausen in 1950 it was changed to steel. The basic Type 356 remained in production until 1965

PORSCHE 356 SPEEDSTER

THE PORSCHE SPEEDSTER was a curious car: its basic layout had the engine 'in the wrong place'. It sold only in small numbers when it was readily available in the mid-1950s, yet when Porsche stopped making the Speedster, enthusiasts howled in rage. Porsche were left wondering why they had not bought the model when it was available and have never stopped marvelling at the way prices of secondhand examples have soared and the number of replicas has multiplied.

The Speedster's origins can be traced straight back to the beginnings of the firm of car makers called Porsche. Professor Ferdinand Porsche had designed some wonderful machines, including the German Volkswagen 'people's car', before the war, but was languishing in a French jail soon after. His son, also called Ferdinand, but better known as Ferry, raised money to bail him out by designing the Cisitalia racing car for an Italian industrialist.

With Cisitalia's Fiat-based road cars for inspiration, Ferry Porsche began to design the first road car to bear his family's name. Supplies of mechanical components in his native Austria were scarce after the war, so the car was built from available materials . . . secondhand Volkswagen parts. The first Porsche, completed in 1948, had a space frame with its Volkswagen engine reversed in a mounting ahead of the rear wheels, rather than behind them. The beautifully streamlined body, designed by Erwin Kommenda, was in many ways like a Volkswagen. This tiny car was very light and performed well, being intended chiefly for racing. It was good for publicity, but the market for such devices was limited, so work went on at the same time to produce a touring car. This version of Porsche design project number 356 stuck more closely to the original Volkswagen concept.

To save money on the skilled labour needed to build a complex tubular frame, it had a platform chassis. The air-cooled engine was also mounted behind the rear axle to give more room inside the body, which was along similar lines to that of the Volkswagen. This extreme rearward concentration of weight made the touring car more tail-happy, but the old professor said that luggage accommodation was more important.

Porsche engineers have been wrestling with the problems of having so much weight at the back ever since, as competition versions continue with the power unit in the theoretically perfect central position. The rear engine did, however, endow the Porsche 356, as it became known, with exceptionally good traction on the rough roads which abounded in Europe immediately after the war, and gave it nimble handling in skilled hands. In fact, it was so lively with its low weight and supple all-independent suspension that good drivers could swing its tail round hairpin bends with great dexterity.

The 356 – in coupé or cabriolet form – had such a slippery shape that high speeds were attainable. They were also very reliable cars because their basic mechanical parts were subject to little stress, and as such became favourite competition vehicles in rallies and early sports car races.

Production built up slowly from an old sawmill at Gmünd, Austria, for an eventual move to Prof Porsche's pre-war headquarters in Stuttgart, West Germany. By March 1951, 500 Porsches had been produced and soon after high-performance versions of the 356 were racing at Le Mans. Old Professor Porsche lived long enough to see them win their class in the great 24-hour race. When he died he left his son Ferry to run the company with the family of his daughter, Louise Piech. As ever more spectacular competition cars were built, the touring cars were

modified so much that they bore very little resemblance to Volkswagens other than in appearance and basic layout.

They sold well on their reputation for durability and high performance, achieved by the competition cars, particularly on the West coast of America where there were enough customers who were not deterred by a price approaching that of an average Cadillac. One dealer, the Austrian-born Max Hoffman, was particularly successful, raising his Porsche sales from three in 1950 to several hundred – a third of the factory's rapidly expanding total production – in 1954.

During those three years, the Porsche 356 received all manner of improvements, but Hoffman remained convinced that the styling was wrong. So he persuaded Porsche to build him a special-bodied 356 roadster along the lines of successful British sports cars like the M.G. TC and Jaguar XK120. This had a normal Porsche nose with an abbreviated tail and lower-cut doors, and bore the name America Roadster. These bodies were made from aluminium on a small scale because it was expected that they would appeal chiefly to customers who wanted minimum weight and maximum visibility for racing. As such they sold quite well in 1952, and continued to do so as Porsche raised the engine capacity from an initial 1100 cc to 1500 cc, with the option of far more powerful four-cam racing units.

Such was the relative success of the American Roadster that it went into larger-scale production, emerging as the Speedster in 1954. This stark little machine became one of the world's best-loved cars and still symbolises what Porsche motoring means to many thousands of people, especially Americans. There was no wasted space, and consequently no excess weight. The Speedster had a distinctive windscreen that was exceptionally low, like the optional aero screens used for racing on the British sports cars. It also made it look even more like a beetle when its skimpy rag top was erected. The Speedster became everybody's boy racer, as fast and manoeuvrable as a pair of roller skates and even more fun. Hoffman's sales soared with such an attractive little beast to publicise Porsche, but those sales were chiefly of far more luxurious standard 356 coupés and cabriolets. All Porsches cost a lot of money, so first owners generally opted for the more comfortable variants!

Porsche became disillusioned with the Speedster because it did not sell in large enough quantities. This was despite having a price pared to the bone (like its body), which offered them only minimal profit. As a result they discontinued their loss leader in 1958 to a storm of protest and have never been able to make a really cheap, successful, Porsche since, in spite of producing more exotic cars than any other manufacturer.

SPECIFICATION

Country of origin: West Germany.

Manufacturer: Porsche.

Model: 356 Speedster.

Year: 1954.

Engine: 4-cylinder horizontally-opposed, air-cooled, overhead valve, 1488cc.

Transmission: 4 forward ratios, transaxle.

Body: Open, 2 seats.

Wheelbase: 83in (2100mm).

Length: 156in (3950mm).

Height: 48in (1219mm) hood erect.

Width: 66in (1664mm).

Maximum speed: 95mph (153km/h).

Instruments were housed in
an anti-glare pinnacle

V8 engine came in two versions:
    292 cu.in. (9.1:1 comp. ratio)
    312 cu.in. (9.7:1 comp. ratio)

14in (355mm) tyres fitted
to safety rim wheels

FORD THUNDERBIRD

Detachable hard top
with characteristic
'port hole' to aid rear
threequarter vision

Massive tail light
had the reversing
light in the centre.
Rear bumper incorporated
the exhaust tail pipe

FORD THUNDERBIRD

I T HAS BEEN said with some conviction that the best thing about the Ford Thunderbird was its name. A symbol of power, flight and Indian mythology, it was the name of the magical totem pole of the Pueblo warriors who roamed the Wild West. But to Americans, the early Ford Thunderbirds will always be classics because they represented everything that was good – and bad – about their native car industry.

Old Henry Ford's empire was in decline when the U.S. Government shut down car production to concentrate on their war effort in 1942. Piles of invoices were weighed rather than paid as rival executives fought to take control during the founder's ailing years, when his heir apparent, Henry Ford II, was but a young naval officer. He was eventually released early from the services in 1945 to sort out the mess back home in Detroit. It was hardly surprising that the cars which followed during the next five years differed little from 1942 models other than in profitability because they cost more to make. But they sold well because they were new, and Henry Ford II was fully occupied in reorganising his company with a solid backbone of former servicemen.

This youthful management rose to the occasion when sales, inevitably, slumped betweeen 1951 and 1952 as the American market for new cars reached saturation point. The only worthwhile trend that had emerged in the 1940s was a predilection by ex-servicemen for more sporting machines, of the type produced in Europe by M.G., Jaguar and Porsche. This desire for cars that were exciting as well as practical had been identified, discussed and mentally assimilated as early as 1951, when General Motors and Ford started working on 'sporty' prototypes. It needed only one – General Motors in this case with

the Chevrolet Corvette and Cadillac Eldorado – to make the first move, for the other to follow, and Ford came out with its first Thunderbird in 1954.

The prototype's reception, at the early season Detroit Auto Show, was rapturous. It had everything a true-blue American needed, except a name. A formal competition to christen the new vehicle won a new suit of clothes for the man from the styling department who came up with 'Thunderbird'. It appealed to the Americans of the day who loved anything new that you could show off. It meant more than cash in the bank, because most folks were still used to being quite hard up. As a result, the first production Thunderbird, a '55 model produced in September 1954, sold well at $3000 (£2000) because it was almost $400 (£260) cheaper than the rival Corvette.

It was a two-seater drophead coupé which, although it weighed one and a quarter tons – 1285kg – was the smallest American Ford built for decades. And if that did not say enough about the American car industry at the time, its dramatic lack of technical innovation confirmed it. The Thunderbird had been able to progress from prototype to production in only a few months because it was largely composed of components from other Ford cars.

Fortunately, however, the engine was the best part: a brand-new overhead valve V8, which in initial 'Law Enforcement' form produced 160bhp against the 130bhp norm, and was quickly raised to 193 bhp for a three-speed manual version and 198bhp for a two-speed automatic, both with gearchange on the steering column. The suspension was standard wallowing Ford sedan, but with a burble that only a V8 could produce. Customers were queuing up for the Thunderbird.

Its styling was absolutely American, as a luxurious two-seater 'personal' coupé that cost twice as much as a regular sedan, and was heavily decorated with chrome. Advanced technology was limited to a tinted Perspex panel behind the instrument nacelle which was meant to catch all available light and make the speedometer glow. It was unfortunate that in areas of strong sunlight, such as in Southern California and Arizona, the magnified rays frequently melted the speedometer needle. 'That's the kinda' problem you get with fast cars,' said owners happy in the knowledge that their V8 would never boil up like a Jaguar's undercooled straight-six.

As Ford executives secretly planned a longer, lower, wider four-seater Thunderbird as big as their sedans and commanding the same sort of purchase price, they used the '56 model as an experiment to see if they could sell safety to the 'great American public out there'. It had a brand-new deep-dish steering wheel, padded dashboard and optional seat belts, as well as dual exhaust pipes routed through the over riders. The safety aspects fell flat in the market place, but that great public out there loved the exhaust pipes, which reminded them of a Porsche. No matter that Porsche had been forced into this emergency measure by a notable lack of ground clearance: the average American looked upon such pipes as the height of fashion.

The spare tyre was also mounted 'continental-style'

behind the rear bumper, with the excuse that it liberated more space in an already vast luggage boot. The fact that its overhanging weight made the handling an even more colourful exercise than that of a Porsche was of no account. The Thunderbird was a safe car with its new steering wheel and optional portholes to improve visibility through the blind sides of its hardtop.

In the summer of its second facelift, the Thunderbird acquired fins. They were reasonably restrained and worked better on the '57 model than on most of its competitors. In fact, that Thunderbird was a positive beauty when viewed alongside the gigantic four-seater introduced for 1958. In retrospect, this was a perfectly ugly 'beast'. It was even recognised as such by many who promptly dubbed it the Squarebird, with its gaping chrome-plated grille, and intergalactic tail fins. But it was just what the American public wanted at the time, as the original G.I. buyers of the two-seater Thunderbird had by now acquired families.

It was not until years later when middle-aged folk thought back with nostalgia to their youth that they realised what they had lost and they yearned again for the 'sporty' cars like those first Thunderbirds, which had been described at the time as a Seventh Heaven on Wheels, Enchantment Unlimited and most often, as A Personal Car of Distinction. You couldn't say that about a family car with four seats!

SPECIFICATION

Country of origin: United States of America.

Manufacturer: Ford.

Model: Thunderbird.

Year: 1957.

Engine: V8 cylinder, overhead valve, 5769cc.

Transmission: 3 forward ratios automatic only, live rear axle.

Body: Open, 4 seats.

Wheelbase: 149in (3785mm).

Length: 214in (5436mm).

Height: 58in (1473mm).

Width: 72in (1829mm).

Maximum speed: 100mph (161km/h).

Facel Vega Excellence — so pricey
that only 156 were ever made

Pillarless 4-door saloon
with centre-opening doors
that latched onto two
small lugs built into
the sills

Cruciform chassis was designed
by the Briton Lance Macklin

Genuine wire wheels
were available as an
alternative to the 'styled'
dummy ones

FACEL VEGA HK500

THE FACEL VEGA HK500 was a gloriously defiant motor car, redolent of the age before air conditioning and air travel, when incredibly wealthy Parisians drove down to the South of France in Bugatti, Delahaye and Hispano-Suiza grand touring cars, to escape the unpleasant climate of the city in mid-summer.

As air technology advanced, such people spent more time in their elegant city apartments, or flew away on holiday. Most of the great French marques were dead, or dying on their feet, when the first Facel Vega appeared.

It was created by Jean Daninos, who made special bodies for cars such as the French Fords, Panhards and Simcas. Early experiments shown at the Paris Salon in 1950 encouraged him to build his own grand touring car, using the lazy power and torque of an American engine in a chassis full of European character. No matter that the French government frowned on anything imported and required him to export five out of every eight cars he built with a foreign engine; no matter that French taxation laws had all but killed off a native industry producing great luxury cars: like so many before him, Daninos thought he could succeed where others had failed.

He chose the biggest and best power unit money could buy for his car: Chrysler's famous 180bhp hemi-headed V8 with its excellent Torqueflite automatic gearbox. But the American practice of using only three gears in manual adaptations was unthinkable for a European machine, so a four-speed box from France was offered, along with a British Salisbury rear axle of unimpeachable quality. The same French cog maker from Pont-à-Mousson, only a few miles from the old Bugatti works, supplied a state of the art cam and roller steering box with equally-

traditional finned light alloy drum brakes. It was unfortunate that these brakes did little to arrest the progress of those first Facels, although that was not unusual in 1954 as new lines in all-enveloping coachwork shrouded the drums from cooling air. The steering was heavy and vague, but so was that used on most contemporary cars. The tubular steel chassis was far from sophisticated, but quite good by comparison with others.

None of that mattered when the Facel Vega's bodywork was revealed. It was extraordinarily attractive, featuring a bold central grille set between elegant ears, with lights clustered vertically on the wing edges. Rear lights set on the top corners of the back wings established another trademark, along with a pillarless coupé roof and strong baselines around the bottom of the body.

Despite its size – 15 feet (4.57m) long and nearly 6 feet (1.8m) wide – Chrysler's mighty hemi could propel this luxury liner to almost 120mph (193km/h) and provide startling acceleration. All France was gripped with excitement at the sight of such a magnificent car. But few Frenchmen laid hands on Facel Vegas as they emerged in 1955, mostly for export, at the rate of one a week from Daninos's factory in Colombes.

It was easy to change the specification of a car produced in such small quantities as every one was, in effect, individually made. Thus, as ever more powerful Chrysler engines were marketed, they were soon fitted to Facel Vegas. The first cars became known retrospectively as FV1s, the FV2 having a 250bhp V8 engine with a higher compression ratio as better petrol became generally available. This led to the FV2B with a 5.4-litre engine giving 285bhp. It was at this point that the hard-pressed brakes were fitted with a servo to help slow these very heavy cars.

Such was the elegance, quality and very high price

of the Facel Vega that it was soon compared to the products of Rolls-Royce. Daninos was overjoyed and celebrated by stretching his chassis by all of 2ft (61cm) for a pillarless four-door Facel Vega called the Excellence. When fitted with an even larger 6.4-litre V8 in 1956 it proved capable of 125mph (200km/h) making it one of the fastest big saloons in the world, although it remained one of the slowest to stop.

In fact, even Daninos became alarmed at the lack of braking ability, but reasoned that if drum brakes were good enough for the reactionary Enzo Ferrari, they were good enough for his cars. He compromised, therefore, by reducing the size of the Excellence's engine to a mere 5.9 litres, which lopped only a few miles per hour off the top speed and did nothing to make it safer.

The chassis of the Excellence was then shortened in 1958, bringing it nearer to the size of a FV2B, resulting in a new two-door pillarless coupé, the HK500. A dramatic reduction in weight eased the braking problem as long as drivers did not attempt to use the top speed of around 140mph (225km/h). Daninos also turned a blind eye to the fact that the Michelin X tyres, fitted as standard, were only rated as safe up to 120mph (193km/h). In 1960, however, he bowed to the inevitable and changed the long-suffering drum brakes for discs on both the HK500 and last series of Excellence four-doors. The result was a boom year in which more than 200 Facel Vegas were built, still mostly for export, with Britain as the chief market due to the enthusiastic efforts of importer George Abecassis.

Overwhelmed by such success and the reception from abroad for what were now truly excellent cars, Daninos decided to try to crack the French market. The only practical way was to build his own engine, as a Facel Vega could hardly be called exclusive with the same power unit as a Citroën or Renault. And the only way to justify such a costly exercise was to spread the development costs over volume sales. This meant building Facel Vegas in sufficient quantity for the engine to be kept exclusive to his cars. In 1961, Daninos therefore, produced the Facellia, a scaled-down HK500 using an advanced twin overhead cam engine in keeping with the marque's glamorous image. Unfortunately, this engine suffered from a lack of finance, and resulting paucity of model development so that the car proved no more dependable than the early brakes. Despite being revamped as the Facel II, the leaf-sprung chassis of the HK500 was also beginning to look very dated.

Facel's fortunes started to crumble as the Facellia – renamed the Facel III – acquired a reliable, but less than romantic, Volvo engine and no more money could be spared to improve the big coupés' chassis. By late 1964 Facel Vega was no more, killed like the great French grand touring cars before it, by a short-sighted taxman.

SPECIFICATION

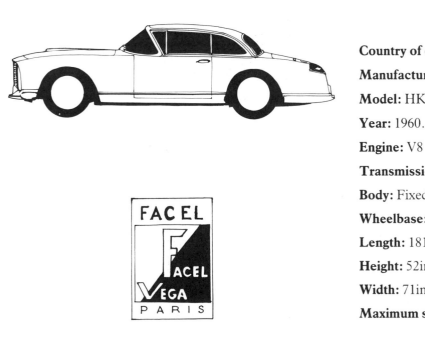

Country of origin: France.

Manufacturer: Facel Vega.

Model: HK500.

Year: 1960.

Engine: V8 cylinder, overhead valve, 6286cc.

Transmission: 4 forward ratios, live rear axle.

Body: Fixed-head coupé, 4 seats.

Wheelbase: 104in (2642mm).

Length: 181in (4797mm).

Height: 52in (1321mm).

Width: 71in (1803mm).

Maximum speed: 140mph (225km/h).

'Binnacle' tachometer
was an optional extra —
car developed maximum
power at 4800 rpm

Epitomising the American glamour convertible,
the Skylark packed a mighty punch, with an
aluminium V8 engine of 190 bhp — and a
four-barrel carburettor

BUICK SKYLARK

'Four on the floor' manual transmission was available in addition to standard automatic

THE HEART OF every car is its engine and this was especially true of the massive V8s which put their weight behind the collective description, Detroit Iron. The sheer size of these engines could be contained only in veritable juggernauts that grew bigger and heavier until forward-thinking individuals began to realise there might be other ways of conveying one person for most of the time and rarely more than four in total.

Such heretical doctrines could be cheerfully ignored until the Land of the Free started to run out of parking space and the Great American Automotive Industry was forced suddenly to start making sensible cars. By the Fall of '59 there was revolution in the air as Chevrolet fielded their Corvair with a rear-mounted, air-cooled, engine, transaxle, independent suspension on all four wheels and an ultra-low profile. Chrysler countered with the decidedly reactionary Plymouth Valiant as Ford forged ahead with the Falcon and the American Motors Corporation with the Rambler Classic. In fact, AMC's president, George Romney, predicted that within three years the revolution would have taken such a hold that more than half the cars from Detroit would be compacts, whereas three years before no self-respecting American buyer would be seen dead in one.

It was hardly surprising that such a revolution spawned technological advances, none more than the world's first all-aluminium production engine used in the Buick Special and Oldsmobile F-85 of 1960, and which was offered as a speculative option in the Pontiac Tempest, normally powered by a leviathan cast iron four-cylinder.

The advantages in weight reduction and efficiency that resulted from the use of aluminium in preference to iron for major castings such as the cylinder heads and block had fascinated engineers for years. The American firm Marmon used it in their Model 34 of 1916 and again with their legendary 200bhp V16 in 1930. The Aluminium Company of America – Alcoa – experimented with an alloy V8 in 1917 and commissioned the noted British engineer Laurence Pomeroy to design several all-aluminium cars after that. They adapted Pontiac components to run in alloy castings in 1942 and Kaiser-Frazer built several aluminium V6 and V8 engines in 1950.

Buick – which had provided the very foundation of General Motors – followed up with an aluminium V8 in their Le Sabre and XP-300 show cars of 1951. This engine, with hemispherical combustion chambers and a Roots-type supercharger produced 300bhp from a substantially similar capacity to Buick's new power unit. But like the single overhead cam aluminium V8 in the La Salle II show car of 1955, it was not a realistic production proposition. General Motors were still finding, like everybody else, that it was all very well designing and building the odd exotic engine, but when it came to hard-nosed business considerations in which cost was of paramount importance, a more conventional specification went into production.

The brave new Buick made it in 1960 because careful analysis revealed that there were bigger potential savings in a bodyshell and suspension that did not have to support so much weight than in the extra cost of making such a jewel of an engine. The major problem with the biggest – and therefore heaviest – component, the cylinder block, had always been how to provide a cylinder wall that was

compatible with hard-wearing pistons and rings. Although intensive research had gone into possible solutions such as high-silicon alloys, metal spraying and plating, none were as reliable as old-fashioned cast iron. Then Lancia and BMW in Europe demonstrated that such engines could work with wet-sleeve designs produced in low volume. The General's engineers were interested, but decided that such a system would never be foolproof and would suffer sealing problems while being serviced by amateur mechanics. It was also very expensive.

But it set their casting department thinking and it was not long before they came up with the idea of machining cast iron liners internally in the normal manner and leaving them with a rough finish on the outside. These liners were then inserted in the aluminium casting's mould so that when the alloy cooled and shrank they were permanently fixed in place with no sealing problems. The same process was used for sinking cast iron valve seats into the cylinder heads.

The rest of the car built around this 3.5-litre V8, which weighed only as much as a 1.5-litre cast iron engine, was relatively mundane. The Special grew a little larger in 1961 and was joined by a vinyl-topped Skylark coupé which looked a good deal better, so much so that most people have forgotten that it was the first mass-produced car to have such a gem of an engine. The General showed signs of forgetting it too when the Special received America's first V6 (a cast iron one this time) in 1962, the Skylark soldiering on with the alloy engine for another year.

Not that there was anything wrong with the engine. Quite simply advanced technology fever had such a firm grip on the General's casting works that they quickly discovered more accurate ways of working with iron. The pace of achievement over those years was such that they reduced iron blocks to an altogether more realistic weight.

Racing folk were nothing like as fickle, favouring the Buick engine for all manner of applications, especially competition boats where weight was exceptionally important. It just so happened that a weekend racer's Skylark engine was standing in the corner of a shipping company's office when a salesman from the British firm Land-Rover dropped by to discuss using their rugged engines in hire boats. As he stumbled against this delightful little V8, he realised it was just what Rover needed to give their ageing saloons a new lease of life.

The rights to produce this redundant engine were bought for a song, together with an ace American development engineer to improve it. In revitalised form it has gone on to power everything from sports cars to Range Rovers – the best engine British Leyland ever had – and started rumours recently that the General wanted to buy it back, now that weight and economy are of paramount importance, through the Company's bid for part of the Leyland empire.

SPECIFICATION

Country of origin: United States of America.

Manufacturer: General Motors.

Model: Buick Special.

Year: 1960.

Engine: V8 cylinder, overhead valve, 3533cc.

Transmission: 3 forward ratios, live rear axle.

Body: Saloon, 5 seats.

Wheelbase: 112in (2845mm).

Length: 188in (4775mm).

Height: 53in (1334mm).

Width: 71in (1811mm).

Maximum speed: 105mph (169km/h).

Glass fibre body was designed by Peter Kirwan-Taylor
and developed for production by Frank Costin
and John Frayling. The car was only 46in (1168mm)
high and weighed 1465lb (660kg) — with
5 gallons (22.7 litres) of fuel

Instruments
included an 8000rpm
tachometer and a
140mph (225km/h)
speedo

LOTUS ELITE

1216cc engine with twin
H4 SU carburettors developing
83 bhp at 6300 rpm. This
Coventry-Climax engine
was derived from a
fire-pump unit designed
to rev instantly from
cold to 5000 rpm

LOTUS ELITE

Suddenly one summer the world's most beautiful grand touring car was conceived. It was the creation of a young accountant called Peter Kirwan-Taylor and a friend of his who was to become the greatest post-war car designer, Colin Chapman. Only a year or so before that fateful summer of '57, they were to be seen in spartan open-topped sports cars, Chapman with his bathtub-bodied Lotus Mark 6 and Kirwan-Taylor with a far more attractive version clothed in coachwork he had designed himself.

But they soon grew out of such anti-social contraptions, no matter how well they drove. Chapman still inspired avid followers to build such cars for next-to-nothing in sheds behind his father's pub. Such activities helped to finance far more advanced Lotus racing cars, the glory of their success being payment enough for Chapman's enthusiastic helpers.

Kirwan-Taylor was different. He did not actually work for Chapman; he was more of an equal, coming from the same mental mould. They both fancied an exclusive grand touring car to show they were on the way to the top of their chosen professions. No matter that neither of them had the money to buy a Porsche or an Alfa Romeo . . . they would make the car themselves.

Ever wiser when it came to investment, Kirwan-Taylor suggested building just one, using the space frame of Chapman's latest racing car, the Lotus Eleven. Then perhaps they could build a few replicas if there were enough people with the money to buy them. Ever more adventurous, Chapman suggested building them by the thousand to make more money.

As Kirwan-Taylor doodled away at the loveliest lines ever to grace such a car, Chapman showed his

real genius. He dispensed with the chassis, incorporating the engine, transmission, steering and suspension mounting points in the bodyshell, which would be made, not of inherently heavy metal, but of the magical new glass fibre, which ought to weigh less. Chapman, who had trained as a stress engineer, saw no reason why this brittle material should not be made strong enough for his purpose. Already he had proved himself as clever as the entire Mercedes engineering team by building his Mark 6 around a space frame at the same time as they were producing their Gullwing. Now he would forge ahead with the world's first plastic car.

Kirwan-Taylor's purity of line was honed to perfection by one of Chapman's part-timers, aerodynamicist Frank Costin from the nearby De Havilland aircraft factory. The result was the first Lotus Elite with a poise and grace which has never been equalled, and never likely to be, as myriad new regulations complicate car design.

Chapman's mechanical contribution was as brilliant as his overall conception. Not only was the body very light but it was strong enough where it mattered, the glass fibre base of varying thicknesses being strengthened by tiny metal inserts. The delicate suspension from his racing cars demonstrated Chapman's theory that a minimum of material, stressed properly would perform better than any excess. Thus the Elite not only had dainty 'legs' but dispensed with contemporary convention by using the lightest tyres Chapman could extract from their manufacturers. His reasoning was as sound as it was simple as he roared at one customer who wanted beefy racing tyres: 'You don't go dancing in clodhoppers.'

And so the Elite ran rings round the weighty opposition, just like the Lotus Eleven racers which

set new standards in sensuous handling, rendering the blood-and-thunder sports car of the 1950s obsolete. The Elite also became the first production car to use the Coventry-Climax engine that had found favour in sports racers like the Eleven and was significant in itself. This marvellous little unit represented a triumph of native British improvisation in that it had originally been designed to power fire pumps! It took the likes of Chapman to recognise that it had all the essential qualities of a high-performance unit, with weight pared to the minimum (because it was meant to be carried by hand) and an ability to stand high revs for long periods (because it was intended to run flat out for hours on end fighting fires).

Unfortunately the Lotus Elite was not so durable. Part of the problem was that Lotus and their suppliers were working with a material in its very early stages of development. Another element was that Lotus was under-financed for such an ambitious project. It was all very well raising the money to build racing cars from customers' deposits, then using the profits for future development, but it did not work out that way with the Elite. The deposits generated by the first show model in 1957 were enough to pay for the materials, but not for instance, for the new factory needed to produce a large number of cars nor to finance exports on which payment was delayed. A third factor was that the workforce was still largely unskilled even as production reached full swing in 1960.

As a result, Elites worked wonders on the track when mechanics outnumbered cars in a racing team, but not when production cars outnumbered skilled labour for servicing. Problems over quality control, or the lack of it, reached massive proportions in America, where customers had been brought up on foolproof cars rather than backyard specials like many British enthusiasts. Rectification costs broke the early importers and nearly took Chapman down.

It was then that he showed financial genius equal to his designing ability. Chapman turned the Elite into a kit car like the limited-production Mark 6 before it. His move slashed the price of what had been a fairly expensive little machine, because no purchase tax was payable on cars that customers assembled themselves. Time and again, Chapman's fortunes were retrieved by such inspired financial footwork, as ever more advanced racing cars routed the opposition to make Lotus world champion constructors and their production cars reached maturity.

Unluckily for Lotus, Kirwan-Taylor's career lay in the City of London and he styled no more cars, although he was on hand to offer sound business advice. What could have been the greatest partnership in the world of cars disappeared when Chapman died in 1982, leaving the Elite as a unique reminder of his genius.

SPECIFICATION

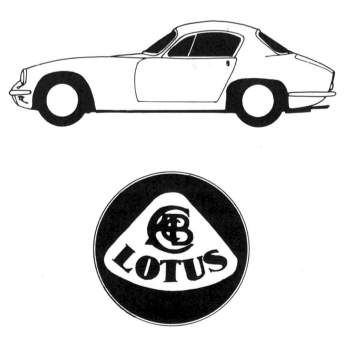

Country of origin: Great Britain.

Manufacturer: Lotus.

Model: Elite.

Year: 1960.

Engine: Coventry climax 4-cylinder in-line, overhead camshaft, 1216cc.

Transmission: 4 forward ratios, body-mounted final drive.

Body: Fixed-head coupé, 2 seats.

Wheelbase: 88in (2242mm).

Length: 148in (3759mm).

Height: 47in (1181mm).

Width: 59in (1505mm).

Maximum speed: 115mph (185km/h).

Zagato 'Z' appeared on all
bodies — even those fitted
and finished at Newport Pagnell

Beneath the aggressive looking body was
a 314 bhp high compression engine
that propelled the car at speeds up
to 152 mph (245 km/h)

ASTON MARTIN DB4GT ZAGATO

Rear end of one of the
lightweight bodies made
and fitted by Zagato
in Italy

ASTON MARTIN DB4GT ZAGATO

JUST AS THE Ulster has always been considered the best pre-war Aston Martin, the Zagato qualifies for this distinction in post-war production because its lightweight body helped overcome the traditional handicaps of a heavy machine. The DB4GT Zagato was also the last of a thoroughbred line that could be traced to the original Aston Martin two-seater sports cars.

When the firm's first saviour, Auguste Bertelli, departed in 1936, the owner's son, Gordon Sutherland, took over in the sound knowledge that future profitability could be ensured only by producing dependable road cars rather than temperamental racing machines. Aston Martin continued with this policy until the war brought further struggles and a new saviour stepped in: tractor magnate David Brown. He learned that another great name in British sporting car circles was having trouble raising the capital to resume post-war production and promptly bought up Lagonda.

One of Aston Martin's principal assets in 1948 was an excellent coil-sprung near space frame, chassis, although the firm lacked a modern engine for its voluptuous post-war sports car, called the DB1 in honour of the new owner. Happily Lagonda's assets included an excellent twin overhead cam power unit that had been designed by none other than W. O. Bentley. It was not long before Brown arranged for the engine from Lagonda's rather exotic saloon to be inserted into Aston Martin's sports car chassis. He then clothed it with a body which was the equal of any Italian grand touring car, designed in house by British stylist Frank Feeley. The DB2 of 1950 then abandoned the marque's image as the 'British Bugatti' to become the 'British Ferrari'.

Success on the race track, particularly at Le Mans,

was reinforced by sports racing versions before the rear end was redesigned to incorporate two tiny rear seats and a top-hinged tailgate which made the DB2/4 the world's first hatchback, and a very sporting one at that.

As DB3, then DB3S, sports racers surged ahead with similar engines, the power of the road cars was stepped up to keep pace with the weight that was a necessary accompaniment to ever-increasing standards of comfort. By the time the DB mark III went into production in 1957, with a 3-litre version of the Lagonda's original 2.6-litre engine, it was more of a fast touring car than anything which could run at Le Mans. Good as it was, others were getting better and Aston Martin needed a new grand tourer with modern styling which could seat two people in great comfort and take four at a squeeze.

Such had been the success of the Italian-inspired lines of the DB2 variants and the DB3S sports racer that it was only natural that Aston Martin should look closely at two particularly attractive show cars built by Touring of Milan on DB chassis in 1956. Although strongly reminiscent of the Lancia Aurelia Spyder of the same era, they were well received in Britain, winning a prize from the Daily Mail newspaper. So Aston Martin turned to Touring to design the bodywork for their new car.

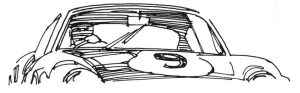

A strong platform chassis proved ideal for Touring's classic superleggera (superlight) method of construction, in which a spider's web of thin steel tubes was erected to support aluminium body panels, thus making a light and rigid structure. Nevertheless, the new car weighed even more than the DB mark III, not only because it was longer, but because the steel floorpan was so massive. But Aston Martin did not worry: they were developing a powerful new 3.7-litre engine which had made their space frame DBR2 sports racing car, the fastest Aston Martin yet. Racing had more than a passing influence on the new

DB4 grand touring car's suspension in that it received wishbones at the front like Aston Martin's emergent DBR4 grand prix challenger to give more precise high-speed handling than the earlier touring cars.

The DB4 of 1958, with its lengthy and luxurious body, set new standards not only of appearance for grand touring cars, but of handling, too, with a mighty 240bhp engine and disc brakes which took it from 0-100mph (0-160km/h) and back to rest in less than 30 seconds during an imaginative publicity stunt. With sensitive new rack-and-pinion steering it was a magnificent car for the road but still too heavy for the track, even when fitted with a more powerful Vantage engine. The potential, however, was evident.

When fitted with a 12-plug racing head and Weber carburettors, more than 300bhp was liberated in a two-seater DB4GT variant which had five inches (125mm) chopped out of the wheelbase to reduce the overall weight by 168lb (76kg) to a still hefty 2800lb (1270kg). Another crack at the earlier DB4 test revealed that this formidable car could accelerate from 0-100mph (0-160km/h) and stop in less than 20 seconds!

Production of this rather wild and temperamental machine was restricted to 75, however, as most customers opted for one of the 1100 far more pleasant standard DB4s built during this period. But there was still a clamour from patriotic enthusiasts intent on showing that a British car could beat the might of Ferrari in GT racing.

To meet this demand, Aston Martin turned to the Italian body builder Zagato, famed for their skimpy racing bodies. Between 1960 and 1961, 19 DB4GT chassis were sent to Italy for ultra-light Zagato bodies, every one built by hand and differing in detail from the next. All but one had perspex covers cowling in the headlights, which reduced drag so much that the top speed, with a 314bhp high-compression competition engine, increased from 140 to 152mph (225-245km/h). The odd one out had normal DB4-style front wings, with exposed headlight glasses, because the first owner from Scandinavia wanted to be able to see where he was going in the Land of the Midnight Sun!

In this form the two-seater Aston Martin road car reached its zenith as a dual-purpose racing car. With spartan seats, plastic windows, hardly any upholstery and not a trace of insulation to deaden the scream of an all-alloy engine, and the savage rasp of open-trumpeted carburettors, the Zagato was loud enough to wake the ghosts of Aston Martin enthusiasts long dead.

So much so that when the firm, some twenty years and several saviours later revealed plans for another Zagato, they were swamped with orders for a car that would be an instant classic, on its name alone.

SPECIFICATION

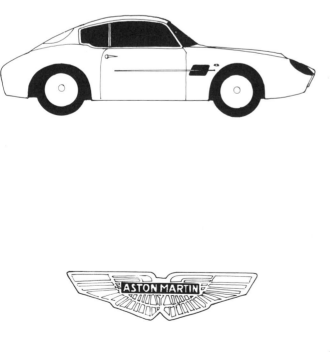

Country of origin: Great Britain.

Manufacturer: Aston Martin.

Model: DB4GT Zagato.

Year: 1961.

Engine: 6-cylinder in-line, twin overhead camshaft, 3670cc.

Transmission: 4 forward ratios, live rear axle.

Body: Fixed-head coupé, 2 seats.

Wheelbase: 93in (2362mm).

Length: 168in (4267mm).

Height: 50in (1270mm).

Width: 65in (1657mm).

Maximum speed: 153mph (246km/h).

In Europe 4.2 litre cars had higher
rear axle ratio, 3.07 : 1. American
models retained the 3.31 : 1 ratio,
giving the edge on acceleration

Easy access to
engine compartment
– note 3 SU
carburettors

4.2 litre engine
producing 265 bhp
at 5400 rpm, giving
maximum speed of
150 mph (241 km/h).
Fuel consumption
17 mpg (6 km/litre)

JAGUAR E TYPE

The Jaguar E type developed through three phases from the 1961 series one to the 1968 series two and the series three in 1971 (series two illustrated)

Disc brakes were fitted to all 4 wheels; 11in (279mm) diameter at front; 10in (254mm) at rear

JUST LIKE THE Jaguars before it, the E type sports car gripped the imagination of a generation, but even more so than the XK120 and SS100. Like the Mini, with its image as a universal saloon car, it became a symbol of social revolution in the Swinging Sixties because, unlike other exotic cars, it was attainable. The E type was far more than just a dream car favoured by pop stars. In relative terms its price was so low that it was temptingly close to what the man or woman in the street could afford. It didn't matter that they would have to break the bank to buy an E type, the stunning appearance and a top speed of 150mph (240km/h) with acceleration to match, made up for all that.

Sir William Lyons was able to take the brave decision to market a production version of his fabulous D type racer at such a competitive price because the E type was one of the last sports cars to be built, without restrictions being imposed by environmental regulations in its main market, the United States. The Land of the Free was still a land of liberty then, with no overall speed limit and precious few safety regulations.

The Jaguar E type also showed what an enlightened leader Lyons could be. Everybody knew he was one of the most significant stylists in the world, yet he himself was not responsible for the E type's incredibly successful shape. That honour fell to his aerodynamicist, Malcolm Sayer, who had redesigned the C (for competition) version of the XK120 as the D type in 1954 using a body like the fuselage of a fighter plane for ultimate efficiency.

This was the car which outran everything else to win at Le Mans three times in succession between 1955 and 1957. It set the sales of Jaguar saloons and sports cars using the same XK engine on a pinnacle, particularly in the affluent areas of America. When the final development of the XK theme, the 150 started to show its age, as a rather fat cat filled with the more luxurious equipment demanded by the American market, Lyons knew better than to change such a distinctive shape for its successor. He was an even more brilliant businessman than stylist and knew when to leave well alone: he simply took the bold step of using the E type to rejuvenate the sports car line. Like the D type, it was as lithe and slim as any 'young-thinking' person would want to be.

Beneath the gloriously long bonnet there was the same 3.8-litre XK engine – rated at 265bhp – which had powered the much heavier top-of-the-range XK150S. But not only was the E type's body far sleeker and better streamlined, it handled far better because, when it was introduced in the spring of 1961, it was the first Jaguar with independent rear suspension. This reassuringly strong system was as efficient as the monocoque and subframes which carried it, having been developed on prototype D types by one of the original factory firewatchers, chief engineer William Heynes.

Although the roadster will always be the absolute classic, a fixed-head version – made with only two seats like the D type – was so outstandingly beautiful that it also sold well.

Meanwhile Lyons showed that he had not changed his philosophy. Once the new mechanical feature, the rear suspension, had been established on the E type, it was introduced in the saloon car line into a massive new six-seater called the Mark X, aimed head-on at America. The interior of this car was as big as that of any American rival, but its graceful lines disguised this, and the fact that it handled better and went faster than anything from Detroit was lost on the vast majority of ordinary Americans. They had been brought up on a homespun philosophy that there was no substitute for cubic inches when it came to status. The Mark X sold reasonably well, with the medium-sized Mark 2 range, but the E type was still the shining star in Jaguar's range.

The only way in which the largest American saloons could match the Mark X's performance was in acceleration with 0-60mph (0-96km/h) figures vital to potential customers squaring up for traffic light drag races. Automatic gearboxes, much in favour in such saloons, also worked better with a great deal of torque, so the XK engine was revamped into a 4.2-litre form to provide the goods. It was not feasible to keep the 3.8-litre version – which revved faster and was inherently better for a sports car – just for the E type, for reasons of production economy. But a new all-synchromesh manual gearbox worked so sweetly, although it absorbed a little more power, that the 4.2-litre E type which followed in 1964 was still outstandingly attractive and just as fast.

Gradually small-town politicians in America established an environmental bandwagon which led to stringent new safety laws there. This movement was encouraged by the reactionary overweight design of the average car from Detroit. It was easy to convince a worried public that the first priority was for cars to be built to withstand mighty impacts (from concrete blocks for the purpose of safety tests), rather than

force US manufacturers to improve handling and brakes to the standards already attained by European cars like Jaguars, even though these were better equipped to avoid accidents in the first place.

A nauseating smog over Los Angeles and other parts of California lent weight to the arguments of environmentalists who claimed that this was caused entirely by the fumes from car exhausts. Subsequent analysis revealed that only a small percentage could be attributed to this source, but the damage had already been done.

It was high-performance cars like Jaguars which suffered the most, slowed by power-sapping anti-emission devices and weighed down with ever-heavier bumpers. First the E type lost its purity of line, culminating in a second series which accommodated such regulations in 1968, and then it became fatter and softer as the series three in 1971. It was the XK150 story all over again, suffering now from features dictated by Americans who did not even buy the cars, although it got its performance back with a 5.3-litre V12 cylinder that was to power the best saloon cars in the world.

Eventually, ever more draconian safety regulations meant that the E type's still sleek nose and tail could crumple badly when it was chained to the ground in the path of a concrete block on a steel sled travelling at 30mph (50km/h). Even Jaguar's Big Cat could not survive *that* in 1974.

SPECIFICATION

Country of origin: Great Britain.

Manufacturer: Jaguar.

Model: E type roadster.

Year: 1970.

Engine: 6-cylinder in-line, twin overhead camshaft, 4235cc.

Transmission: 4 forward speeds, frame-mounted final drive.

Body: Open, 2 seats.

Wheelbase: 96in (2438mm).

Length: 175in (4445mm).

Height: 48in (1219mm) hood erect.

Width: 66in (1664mm).

Maximum speed: 135mph (217km/h).

Alloy centre-lock
wheels by Borrani

Quadruple exhausts from the
3-litre V12 engine

FERRARI 250GTO

Only 40 genuine GTOs were
built and only 33 had this
classic body shape
designed in-house
at Ferrari

Massive gearshift emphasises
the car's competition ancestry.
The engine produced 300 bhp
like the Testa Rossa
sports racer

FERRARI 250GTO

THE 250GTO IS regarded as one of the greatest classics because it was the last front-engined racing car built by Enzo Ferrari which could be driven on the road. As a result it has always been something of a symbol because roads represent an escape to a better life, and chariots – with their horses at the front – the quickest way to get there.

As Ferrari, whose career in the top echelons of motor racing started in 1923, epitomises the sport, so the engine has always been the heart and the soul of his cars. It was fitting that his greatest engine, the V12 cylinder designed by Gioacchino Colombo in 1946, should reach its culmination in the GTO. Its status was enhanced by the red crackle finish on its cam covers, emphasising that this power unit was the Testa Rossa, or red head, the life-blood of the business.

In an equally symbolic manner, the 250GTO was born out of a holocaust when 82 people were killed in motor racing's worst-ever crash at Le Mans in 1955. Numerous races for the exotic sports prototypes which contested such events were cancelled in the aftermath. Considerable concern centred on the fact that wealthy enthusiasts, who were not necessarily good drivers, could go racing in such machines.

Regulations were changed to encourage events for grand touring cars, which were expected to be slower and less dangerous to drive. At the same time, the prototypes – which could be built only in small quantities because they were so expensive – were not banned because they were necessary to pull in the crowds. A key factor in the new regulations decreed that at least 100 grand touring cars needed to be produced to qualify for international competition.

The idea was that the wealthy amateurs would turn to these cars while more skilled professional drivers handled the prototypes.

The new regulations worked well to begin with until Ferrari started winning everything with a prototype called the Testa Rossa, named after his famous 300bhp engine. Spectators became bored and regulations were revised for the world endurance racing championship which they contested so that GT cars replaced prototypes. The organisers' idea was to give other makers a chance of winning, and so restore the spectacle of closely-fought contests between different makes. Not for the first time, the sport's ruling body had reckoned without the experience of Enzo Ferrari.

His existing 250GT production cars had dominated competitions such as the Tour de France, a combination of road stages and races, but were not fast enough to win the world endurance events like Le Mans. This was chiefly because they had less highly-tuned engines than the Testa Rossa to make them cheaper and easier to drive, and square-cut noses to keep them cool on slow road sections, which reduced their maximum speed. What was needed to win the world championship was a Ferrari 250GT with a Testa Rossa engine and a wind-cheating nose.

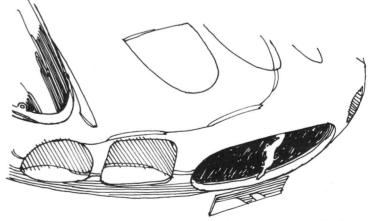

As with the prototype racers, it was easy to find customers to buy one or two, but the cost was such that there was no likelihood of selling the 100 required under GT racing regulations. But Ferrari built the car anyway, with an even more expensive dry sump version of the Testa Rossa engine that enabled the bonnet line to be lowered. Ventilation flaps were also cut in a sleek new nose in the hope that they could be opened to let in enough air on the rare occasions when the car was travelling slowly. This engine also needed a five-speed racing gearbox rather than the normal four-speed GT unit. But the chassis and suspension were similar to the normal 250GT, even if the engine, gearbox and body bore it little resemblance. Ferrari's rivals complained bitterly that this was really a new car . . . and asked how many had been built.

The organisers had little option but to repeat the question, but with tremendous self-confidence, Enzo Ferrari replied: 'Just a few. It does not matter, these cars are simply 250GTs with a few changes that are unimportant . . . and I have produced more than 100 normal cars since 1954, so that means they qualify for the world championship.' The organisers said, 'that might not be enough to keep your rivals quiet. Could it not be said that you intend to produce 100 of the new cars?' With even greater confidence, Ferrari replied 'No, the market is already saturated because only a few men are capable of handling such machines. If you will not accept this car I will not race again.'

At that time, a world championship would not have been a world championship in spectators' eyes without Ferraris, so – terrified at the prospect of races having to be cancelled through the loss of such spectator attractions – the organisers declared that the new Ferrari was eligible for the world championship. This strange qualifying process was known as 'homologation', translated into Italian as *Omologato*. Thus, the ultimate Ferrari road racer took the name 250GTO, for 250GT-Omologato, as the 1962 world championship season started.

Chief opposition came from cars such as the Aston Martin DB4GT Zagato, which was not quite so far removed from the normal DB4, and Jaguar's lightweight E type, which somehow slipped through the regulations when Jaguar claimed that their steel production cars were prototypes and the dozen E types built with aluminium panels were, in fact, the standard model! Nevertheless, the Ferrari had the best power-to-weight ratio and achieved its objective by winning the world endurance championship.

There was still nothing which could stay with it in 1963, so more were built and they won the title again, with one model equipped with a 4-litre engine to run as a prototype. To add a touch of comedy, a normally partisan crowd at Monza gave all their support to a DB4GT Zagato driven by the Briton Roy Salvadori because Astona Martini, Zagato and Salvadori sounded far more Italian than Ferrari's GTO works driver, Mike Parkes!

Eventually, three even more streamlined 250GTO's ran to capture a historic hat trick in the 1964 world championship and bring the final production run up to 40.

SPECIFICATION

Country of origin: Italy.

Manufacturer: Ferrari.

Model: 250GTO.

Year: 1962.

Engine: V12 cylinder, overhead camshaft, 2953cc.

Transmission: 5 forward ratios, live rear axle.

Body: Fixed-head coupé, 2 seats.

Wheelbase: 102in (2595mm).

Length: 173in (4400mm).

Height: 49in (1245mm).

Width: 66in (1675mm).

Maximum speed: 176mph (283km/h).

Fascia was derived from the more mundane Falcon saloon

Note automatic transmission

'Styled' steel wheel was a popular option in 1965 particularly on GT models

Name 'Mustang' was chosen by John Conley of Ford's advertising agency

Chrome trim on dummy
airscoop for an optional
extra for the customers
who wanted extra
bright work

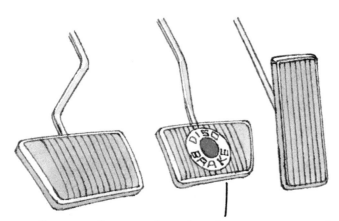

Kelsey-Hayes front disc brakes were a late '65 option;
cars so fitted had a reminder disc on the brake pedal

FORD MUSTANG 289

FORD BUILT A reputation second to none for producing the cheapest and most dependable cars in the world – and then found that reputation to be a massive handicap in a marketplace dominated by a new generation with money to burn. If they were to survive the Swinging Sixties they would have to get rid of their image as producers of boringly reliable cars.

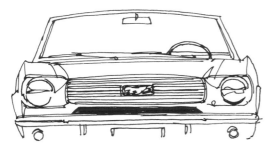

First they tried to buy the greatest high-performance name of all, Ferrari, with a takeover bid for old Enzo's firm, but – like others before them – found it impossible to tie the Commendatore down. So Ford lay siege to the competition world from every conceivable angle, eventually settling for a heavy investment in Colin Chapman of Lotus – the only man that Ferrari recognised as his equal – after discovering that they could not buy him either. Then they stimulated competition among their own executives to promote the new image.

Dynamic sales director Lee Iacocca was the first to respond by creating a car which looked sporty, carried four people and cost less than $2500 (£1700). It harked back to the first Thunderbird as a far smaller car than had become typical of America in the jukebox opulence of the 1950s. Like the early Thunderbird, this was called a personal car, and as such offered an amazing variety of options that meant it really was possible to have a car which was different, even if only slightly, from the one in the drive next door. Thus owners of the bottom-of-the-range 170 cu in (2.8-litre) six-cylinder cars could boast of economy while top notchers with a 289 cu in (4.7-litre) could demonstrate a searing performance, with thousands of variants of trim and mechanical packaging in drop-head or hardtop bodies distinguishing the range in between.

This thrusting new generation was also, paradoxically, nostalgic for the freedom of the Wild West they had never seen and the cowboys who rode the range. So it was hardly surprising that Ford's new car was named after the small, manoeuvrable, hard-fighting horse that all good cowboys rode: the Mustang.

Never has a car hit its market so precisely and so fast. Lee Iacocca's Mustang sold 22,000 on its first day in 1964 and more than 400,000 in its first year of production. It blazed a trail that the opposition had no choice but to follow – General Motors did so with Camaro and Firebird cars named after the Indian side of cowboy games. American Motors went for High School action with the Javelin and Chrysler, after some thought, went for the only line left in leisure activities, Barracuda. But young people, or the young at heart, who bought these models gave them the best name of all: pony cars.

They had to have all the brawn of muscle cars, such as the massive Pontiac GTO, allied to the finer points of a nimbler, more athletic machine, like the Mustang. Such desires were fuelled by a competition programme, under Texan racing driver Carroll Shelby. He not only dressed like a cowboy, but fought like one in Ford's corporate view, creating the AC Cobra (a combination of an English sports car chassis with a Ford V8 engine) which toppled the Ferrari 250GTO in GT racing.

Shelby did much the same with the Mustang for production car racing in the United States. In such events, run by the Sports Car Club of America, competitors were allowed either the engine or the suspension. Changing the engine was the more appealing option to Ford and Shelby because, at the time, Americans tended to measure performance in terms of horsepower rather than handling. Besides, there was more money to be made from selling complicated parts to convert your engine than simple things like new springs for the suspension. In addition, the Mustang's body had been made good and strong in the days before weight-saving became important for economy. Shelby, therefore, followed the same line as he had with the Cobra. With a bit of pushing and shoving, he crammed the biggest and most powerful V8s he could find into Mustang shells, with minimal modifications to the rest of the running gear.

At first these engines took the form of uprated variants of the iron-block 289 which had been made reasonably light by Ford's advanced new thin-wall casting, introduced to save the expense of a Buick-type alloy. Mated with a four-on-the-floor shifter for manual transmission (meaning an ordinary European-style four-speed gearbox rather than a normal American wide-ratio steering column change three-speed, or automatic box), this engine was taken from 271 to 340bhp for the Shelby 350GT. Such machines were highly successful against heavyweights like the Corvette, especially when they received disc brakes in 1965.

The General could not take that lying down and took up the gauntlet in a horsepower race, during which Ford upped Shelby's output with, first, a 390 cu in V8 (of 6.4 litres) in 1966 and ultimately a 428 cu in (7 litre) for the GT500 KR – for King of the Road,

exaggerating its 400 plus horsepower as 500 – by 1969. Inevitably, however, the weight had risen and the distribution, with at least 60 per cent in the nose, was unpleasant, so the original 289 models were still superior.

By that time Shelby's name was better known than Ford's when it came to high performance, so the project was taken in house and the whole range of Mustangs restyled as longer, lower and wider cars. The new design – called the Mach 1 – lost a lot of the relatively lithe attraction of the earlier Mustang, but it still went well with a 351 cu in (5.7 litre) engine as standard against the less sophisticated 289 and 302 which had been used in normal Mustangs.

As for Ford's versions of a Shelby Mustang, the 428 Cobra Jet's 355bhp and 440 lb/ft of torque gave it a lurid performance on the primitive cross-ply tyres with which it was fitted. Bodies continued to expand as far as the Boss Mustang 351 of 1971 before the world's first energy crisis decimated the market for such dinosaurs in 1973. The Mustangs made from 1974 onwards reverted to the smaller body size because, in the interests of economy, they needed less than half the horsepower to haul them along.

As such they were but a pale shadow of the pony cars, with the first lightweight 289 and the disc-braked 350GT the best of the early machines and the GT500KR and Cobra Jet the most awesome leviathans.

SPECIFICATION

Country of origin: United States of America.

Manufacturer: Ford.

Model: Mustang 289.

Year: 1964.

Engine: V8 cylinder, overhead valve, 4736cc.

Transmission: 3 forward ratios or automatic.

Body: Open or closed, 2 seats.

Wheelbase: 108in (2743mm).

Length: 182in (4613mm).

Height: 51in (1295mm).

Width: 68in (1732mm).

Maximum speed: 127mph (204km/h).

1964 Monte Carlo winning
Mini Cooper 'S' driven
by Paddy Hopkirk

Full width facia
incorporated 125mph
(200km/h) speedo, tacho,
twin stop watches, and
a complicated array of
switches controlled many lights

'Les Leston' wood-rimmed
wheel, also note
lengthened throttle pedal

MINI-COOPER 1275S

The car is fitted with 5 auxiliary lamps and a roof lamp as well as the normal headlights, because the main lamps are fitted with iodine vapour single filaments that cannot be dipped

Grill is sawn in half and is quickly detachable. Aluminium plates deflect road spray from the distributor. Accessories include radiator muff and alloy sump guard

MINI-COOPER 1275S

THE MINI IS an absolute classic because nobody has been able to design a smaller car to transport four full-sized people in comfort. It was designed at the beginning of an era when small was considered beautiful, a reaction to big things, which were considered overwhelming, and ugly.

The Mini was conceived in 1956 in response to an oil crisis when supplies of this lifeblood were cut off to the West. The first tangible result in car design was a flood of 'bubble' cars powered by motor cycle engines. Sir Leonard Lord, chairman of the British Motor Corporation, realised that the market needed something better than these bug-like machines and said as much to his chief designer, Alex Issigonis.

Issigonis, who had already demonstrated his brilliance with the Morris Minor, the first British car to sell a million, showed his real genius by turning the Minor's engine round to face east/west instead of north/south. Then he mounted it on top of the transmission and crammed everything under a bonnet far shorter than anything comparable, eliminating the need for bulky intrusions into the interior. The whole package was contained in a 10ft (3.05m) square box, 8½ft (2.6m) of which could be devoted to the occupants because tiny 10in (254mm) wheels took up little room within the perimeter

It was just what the British public wanted – a wholesome symbol of the values held by a nation trying to regain its equilibrium after the Second World War. Small planes and small boats had saved them during that war of still recent memory. Big countries, people and things were dangerous. Small

was secure and affordable. Modesty was seen as a virtue, aggression was concealed. These people rebelled against autobahns, motorways and the American way of life.

After a predictably reserved reception, they recognised the Mini as something quintessentially British. When it eventually found wide public approval, a full year after its introduction in 1959, they discovered that a Mini would fit neatly into a parking space too small for almost any other car. At last they had found a worthy successor to the much-loved Austin Seven.

The Mini also became trendy. At a time of great creative awareness it appealed to young people who fell in love with it not only because it was cheap and dependable, but because it had amazingly safe handling. This meant that in standard form it could out-manoeuvre almost any other car and when 'hotted up' was capable of extraordinary feats.

Racing car manufacturer John Cooper was the first to exploit this ability on a large scale with his Mini-Cooper, produced on a royalty by BMC. Soon these far faster Minis were beating everything in their class on the track, and proving formidable competitors in rallies, despite ground clearance which was limited by such small wheels. It needed only the creation of the higher-powered Mini-Cooper S by the factory competitions department in 1963 to provide a classic giant-killing act. Soon the smallest Mini-Cooper S, with a 970cc engine developed for Formula Junior single-seaters, began to dominate the 1000cc class of international touring car races.

This was the sweetest of all Coopers, having an

engine which revved like a sewing machine. But it was the rougher-running, longer-stroke, Mini-Cooper 1071S that achieved lasting fame in 1964, when Irishman Paddy Hopkirk outran a team of Ford Falcons, powered by engines nearly five times as big, in the Monte Carlo, the world's most glamorous rally. The Americans withdrew, bewildered that such an insignificant little box on wheels could thrash their giants. They never understood the Mini, rejecting it in the marketplace as being beneath their dignity, and failing to realise that it was capable of David-and-Goliath acts in competition because it had such a superior power-to-weight ratio.

By 1965, the Mini-Cooper S engine had grown to 1275cc and all Europe wanted to own one, when Scandinavian star Timo Makinen won the Monte Carlo Rally again. This time 201 of the 237 starters were eliminated, scrabbling for traction in one of the worst blizzards to strike the mountain roads in France. Thanks to its front-wheel-drive, Makinen's Mini ploughed on to become the only car not penalised for losing time on the road. The French were infuriated by the massive defeat of their Citroën. Their anger increased when Makinen arrived late for the formal presentation by their beloved Princess Grace, when his hard-pressed Mini refused to start again!

So they rewrote the rules the next year in the hope that a Mini could never again win their greatest rally.

When Makinen's 1275S led the Mini team into the first three places, they were promptly disqualified – allowing a Citroën to win – because their lights were too bright! The furore that followed filled newspapers and television screens throughout the world and gave the Mini more publicity than any hat-trick of wins. And the 'Monte's' reputation degenerated into that of just another rally.

By then the Europeans' love affair with the Mini had turned into a real passion. Minis were showered with presents, adorned with all manner of accessories, decorations which demonstrated that although the owner belonged to a group of like-minded people, he or she was really an individual too. A new generation of pop stars turned their Minis into limousines and patriotic fans painted their cars in Union Jack stripes to demonstrate that they were 'backing Britain'. A culture developed in which everything became 'mini', from skirts to package holidays and transistor radios.

Other car manufacturers caught up, and the Mini entered the 1970s as just another small car. Its rivals grew larger and more lavish in their appointments for a new age of Super Minis inspired by the decline of larger, better-furnished, cars during the world's first oil crisis. It was then that the Mini came into its own again as an absolute minimum of motor car, and one of the most economical; so much so that it is now the object of a real cult.

SPECIFICATION

Country of origin: Great Britain.

Manufacturer: British Motor Corporation.

Model: Austin-Cooper 1275S.

Year: 1964.

Engine: 4-cylinder in-line, overhead valve, 1275cc.

Transmission: In unit with transverse engine.

Body: Saloon, 4 seats.

Wheelbase: 80in (2032mm).

Length: 120in (3048mm).

Height: 53in (1346mm).

Width: 55in (1397mm).

Maximum speed: 96mph (155km/h).

Instrument panel
included speedo,
tachometer,
oil pressure, water,
temperature, ammeter
and fuel gauges

Concept and body design
was by G.M. design chief,
William L. Mitchell

Positraction limited slip
differential

CHEVROLET CORVETTE STINGRAY

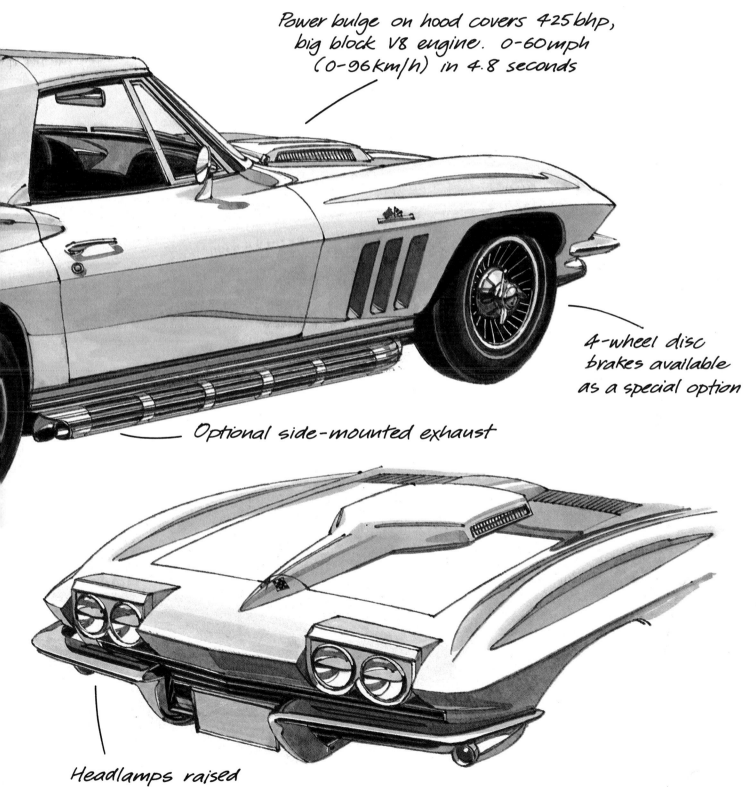

Power bulge on hood covers 425 bhp, big block V8 engine. 0-60 mph (0-96 km/h) in 4.8 seconds

4-wheel disc brakes available as a special option

Optional side-mounted exhaust

Headlamps raised by electric motor

CHEVROLET CORVETTE STINGRAY

For all its good and bad points, the Chevrolet Corvette has always embodied the American concept of a classic sports car. It went into production as the world's first mass-produced plastic car in 1953 and since then has continued to prove that Chevrolets do not have to be boring. The Corvette was the conception of General Motors' stylist Harley Earl and chief engineer Ed Cole, indignant that European sports cars were doing so well in America, even if the General's mundane saloons outsold them 1000 to 1.

They won backing for the project from General Motors' normally very conservative senior executives on the basis that it would be a mobile testbed for advanced technology, as for instance with the body made from the glass fibre which had been used for World War Two patrol craft: hence the name Corvette. General Motors' hierarchy felt safe in the knowledge that anything that might go amiss with a sporty car would not detract in the public's eye from their normal run of stolid saloons.

The Corvette has continued in its testing role to this day, most recently by its pioneering use of plastic leaf springs. But there have been some notable models in the intervening years, not least the Sting Ray series with the early split window and the late 427 power unit which made it one of the most awe-inspiring creations of the muscle car era.

Budgets for Corvette development were never large, particularly in the early days, because it was not seen as a high-volume seller. In fact, one of the reasons for using glass fibre bodywork was that it did not need the heavy investment in tooling associated with mass-produced steel bodies and could be changed quickly as fashion dictated. The rest of the

car would have to come from the corporate parts bin.

Early models looked racy, but had a far from sporting performance because they could only use an ancient straight six-cylinder engine mildly uprated to 150bhp, with a two-speed automatic transmission. Chassis development was limited to a cross-braced box section frame with leaf-sprung back axle, the principles of which dated back to the age of the horse and cart. Despite an enthusiastic reception at the General's travelling Motorama show, the Corvette did not sell well until 1956, after it had received a modern V8 and manual transmission to give it a performance more like that of a sports car.

By then development engineer Zora Arkus-Duntov – a keen competition fan – was gradually extracting more power and torque to give the '56 'Vette, as all-American enthusiasts called it, a top speed of 120mph (193km/h) with acceleration to match, followed by even more spritely performance from a four-speed gearbox in 1957. There was even a competition programme lined up for a Sebring SS prototype, featuring an ultra-lightweight magnesium body, space frame and de Dion rear axle, but the General's rear guard of ageing executives killed the project stone dead when the U.S. National Safety Council proclaimed that racing on the track led to death on the roads.

However, the Sebring SS was successfully remodelled by the General's chief designer, Bill Mitchell, as the Stingray for the less arduous, and presumably safer, amateur production car racing. And in 1962 when the Stingray's racing days were over, Mitchell made it into a road car.

The impact of this machine was immediate: the Corvette's primitive chassis was reworked to operate with independent rear suspension by means of a traditional leaf spring mounted transversely across the chassis. Although the chief advantages of this system were that it was cheap and occupied little space, it did get rid of the axle tramp and oversteer which had plagued previous Corvettes. Totally inadequate drum brakes remained a problem, however, despite being fitted with cast iron linings like a railway engine in a vain attempt to eliminate fade! There were times when safety campaigners were fully justified in castigating the accountants who controlled the General's expenditure on development.

Mitchell's influence also extended to styling, with dramatic effects on the 1963 Sting Ray production car – splitting the name in two words because he had split the back window into two parts! Americans loved this extraordinary coupé and boosted sales by 50 per cent, but the General's corps did not. So the 1964 Corvette Sting Ray lost its split rear window much to Mitchell's disgust, and the 1963 model became an instant classic.

But the fact remained that drivers had a hard time stopping the Sting Ray, especially as engines were growing ever larger and more powerful, ranging from a mere 327 cubic inches (5.3 litres) and 300bhp to the 427 (7 litres) with 425bhp and a massive 465lb/ft of torque for the all-time greatest muscle car in 1966. With a low rear end ratio it was possible to break the gate in a drag race to 60mph (96km/h) in less than 5 seconds (if you did not choke on the swirling clouds of tyre smoke) or, with a rumbling, juddering,

take-off on an ultra-high ratio, it was possible to reach 160mph (257km/h) (in theory, and providing the whole car had not been launched into orbit by bumps no bigger than cigarette packets).

A more conservative ratio between the two extremes was to be recommended, and when this was achieved the Sting Ray became a more 'civilised' car, particularly when it at last received disc brakes for vastly improved stopping power in 1965.

Looming environmental and safety regulations sounded the death knell of the Sting Ray in 1967, and Corvettes became far more boring after that. A longer wheelbase fourth-generation Stingray (all one word now) reached 454 cubic inches (7.4 litres) by 1970, but subsequently lost power due to emission controls after that, bottoming out at 205bhp by 1975 as America and the rest of the western world writhed in the grip of an oil crisis. It was also around 1970 that the masterminds of the Corvette, Cole, Mitchell and Arkus-Duntov, all retired, ending any hope of more advanced concepts.

It was not until 1983 that engineering design perked up and the Corvette entered a fifth generation with its new plastic springs and careful – if not entirely successful – attempts to finally make it handle like a European sports car. So it can be seen that the fabulous 427 Sting Ray of 1966 was the real classic, even if latter-day stylists love the unstoppable '63 model.

SPECIFICATION

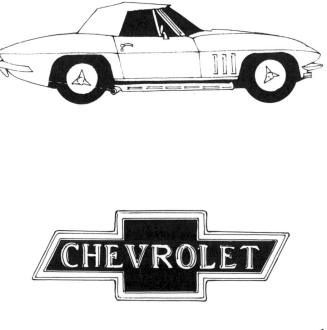

Country of origin: United States of America.

Manufacturer: General Motors.

Model: Chevrolet Corvette Stingray.

Year: 1966.

Engine: V8 cylinder, overhead valve, 5358cc.

Transmission: 3 forward ratios or automatic.

Body: Open or closed, 2 seats.

Wheelbase: 98in (2489mm).

Length: 175in (4453mm).

Height: 50in (1265mm).

Width: 70in (1768mm).

Maximum speed: 129mph (208km/h).

The six-cylinder double overhead camshaft engine was designed by Ing. Giulio Alfieri — it produced 225 bhp at 5200 rpm

Mistrale was first introduced at the Turin Show. Body was designed by Frua and built by Maggiore of Turin. Construction was mostly steel, but doors, bonnet and boot lid were light alloy

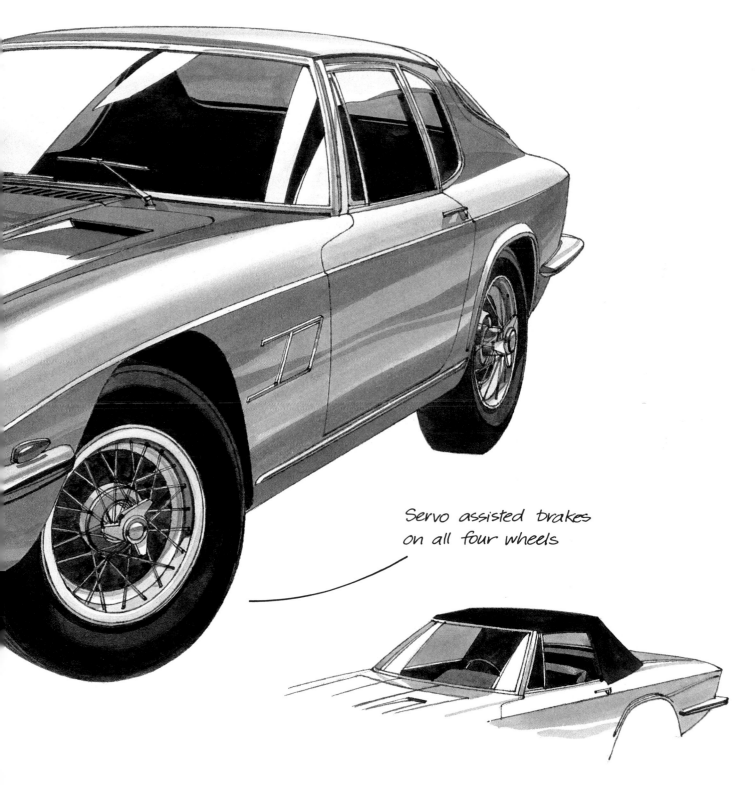

Servo assisted brakes
on all four wheels

MASERATI MISTRALE

MASERATI'S MISTRALE WAS not only a stunning car to look at but also a sad reminder of what might have been. Its conception can be traced to 1956 when Maserati's reputation was at its height after the success of its outstandingly attractive grand prix car, the 250F. Jaguar were selling ever-increasing numbers of production cars as a result of the exploits of their equally beautiful sports racers, so Count Omer Orsi, who ran Maserati, saw no reason why his firm should not benefit in the same way and at a higher price level, because their reputation had been established with the even more glamorous single-seaters.

Chief engineer Giulio Alfieri, therefore, reworked the distinctly Jaguar-like twin overhead camshaft straight six-cylinder engine of the 350S sports racer for larger-scale production in a grand touring car which would produce profits as vast as its appearance was exotic. It had to look even better than a Jaguar under the bonnet to justify a far higher price, so it received two sparking plugs per cylinder (giving it as many as a V12 Ferrari) and those compulsory harbingers of high performance, three twin-choke Weber carburettors.

The chassis, not so easily visible, was a far more straightforward affair. It was made from steel tubing of varying section with no sign of the scientific weight-saving practiced by the likes of Lotus. Maserati were also too small to make much of the running gear in sufficiently profitable quantities, so they bought from a variety of component suppliers: the gearbox and steering gear were made by ZF in Germany, the final drive by Salisbury in Britain, the Girling brakes and clutch – shared with Jaguar – came from Britain too, along with the Alford and Alder independent front suspension much favoured on mass-produced British cars. The age-old half elliptic rear suspension and live axle was exactly what you would expect to find on an American car of the same era.

But the body of the 3500GT, as it was called, was pure Italian, with Touring making the fixed-head coupés and Vignale the convertible Spiders. Disparagers sometimes called these Maseratis Japanese Jaguars, and at other times imitation Ferraris or Aston Martins. But they carried the marque's trident badge on their noses and that was enough to sell as many road cars in 1958 as the previous Maserati production sports models had in seven years. Sales soared from 119 to a peak of more than 500 in 1961 as extraordinary Maserati 'birdcage' sports racing cars swept everything before them in the United States.

By the time the 3500GT had disc brakes on all four wheels and a less tail-happy short wheelbase chassis in 1962, it was quite a good car. It was then that they adopted the early Lucas fuel injection used on later examples of the Jaguar D type sports racers for increased power and a more modern five-speed gearbox from ZF.

Vignale also produced a more futuristic-looking fixed-head coupé, the model, with its four head-lamps, being called the Sebring, in an attempt to woo more American customers. It certainly looked exotic, but the fact remained it was not as fast as an E type Jaguar which cost less than a third of the price. Maserati Birdcages were also going out of fashion on the race track.

The Italian firm countered declining sales by increasing their engine capacity to 3.7 litres for even more power and torque. Then they offered the new power unit in a still shorter chassis, with a superb new body from Frua. The result was a considerable saving in weight, far better acceleration and a top speed approaching that of the Jaguar because the new body had a similar wind-cheating nose. It was intended to be far more appealing to the Americans, because it had a prominent chrome-plated bumper, which subsequently appeared on an E type restyled by Frua's Italian rivals, Ghia!

The real purpose of the grille, however, was to disguise a truly massive air intake designed to avoid the cooling problems that beset Jaguar in some parts of America as a result of the limitations of their beautiful slim-line nose. The back of the Mistrale was equally innovative, featuring a 'goldfish bowl' rear window set in a hatchback, a style which would be copied for years to come. Altogether the appearance was far more elegant than that of the Sebring, which was soon dropped.

The Mistrale then became far more popular with a wealthy clientèle which wanted a car more exclusive than a Jaguar or a Porsche, and one with a body as exotic as any Ferrari. But the number of people who could afford such extravagances, and who remembered the glories of Maserati's past, was declining, so the Mistrale failed to dominate the American market.

The once proud marque faced an almost impossible situation where it could no longer afford the immediate investment needed to produce more advanced cars nor could it bring down the price of the ones it already had.

But it still managed to make more than 800 Mistrale fixed-head coupés and 120 Spiders that some people liked even better, double the number of Sebrings, in the six years to 1970. The last straight six-cylinder cars, made from 1968, even had a full 4-litre engine on the way to a new V8 in a model called the Indy, which represented another attempt to attract those elusive American customers. But that was a heavier car with only 4.2 litres at first and no match for the lighter, shorter Mistrale which came so close to disputing Ferrari's traditional domain.

Now that those six-cylinder Maseratis are no longer available, enthusiasts – particularly in America – have realised what they have lost: a car with all the elegance and finesse that the pony cars, and the muscle cars before them, never had. The tragedy was heightened by the inability of Maserati, whose charismatic history predated Ferrari by more than two decades, to compete successfully on the race track after 1961, and to put into series production cars which were anything like as exotic as the ones that they raced. In reality, what they lacked was a leader with the foresight and organisational ability of old Enzo himself.

SPECIFICATION

Country of origin: Italy.

Manufacturer: Maserati.

Model: Mistrale.

Year: 1967.

Engine: 6-cylinder in-line, twin overhead camshaft, 3692cc.

Transmission: 4 forward ratios, live rear axle.

Body: Fixed-head coupé or open, 2 seats.

Wheelbase: 95in (2400mm).

Length: 177in (4500mm).

Height: 51in (1300mm).

Width: 65in (1650mm).

Maximum speed: 159mph (255km/h).

Engine was mid-ships

Luggage boxes mounted on each side of the silencer

Mighty 4.7-litre V8 engine developed more than 300 bhp

FORD GT40

Car was produced and developed
for Ford by their British factories
In roadgoing form, car was
capable of 0-60mph
(0-96km/h) in 5.3 seconds
and 0-100mph
(0-160km/h) in
11.8 seconds

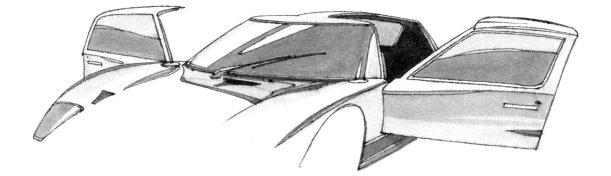

FORD GT40

THE FORD GT40 was more than a classic Le Mans winner, it was the last great endurance racing car also built for use on the road. Everything that followed was totally unpractical for such dual purpose driving, with ever-widening tyres which had to be changed for the rain or would not last in the dry.

Like the AC Cobra, the Shelby Mustang and numerous other competition cars, it was conceived as Ford's 'total performance' marketing package in which the youth market had been identified as the fastest growing sector of demand. The object was to beat the rest of the world, Ferrari in particular, at Le Mans. Henry Ford's determination was intensified by the suspicion that he had been used as a mere pawn in the game which had resulted in Enzo Ferrari getting his firm financed by Fiat as a 'national treasure' which could not be allowed to leave Italy!

Having failed to buy Ferrari, Ford went head hunting in Britain, and hired Colin Chapman to spearhead an attack on the other main objective, Indianapolis. It became increasingly obvious, however, that Chapman – being of an independent mind – could be as difficult to deal with as Ferrari. So Ford executives looked for a more docile version of Chapman who would accept direction from Detroit.

British-born engineer Roy Lunn was sent back to Europe to lead a fact-finding mission to Le Mans and returned with the news that Ferrari were still winning, but that a new Ford V8-engined coupé, built by the British firm Lola, looked promising. So Lola's Eric Broadley was hired to design a new Ford GT with former Aston Martin team chief John Wyer to race it, the whole operation being run by Lunn through a new organisation known as Ford Advanced Vehicles, or FAV for short.

At this time the executives in Detroit knew a great deal about internal politics and producing saloon cars by the million, but not much about building European-style racing cars. Broadley wanted a lightweight monocoque like Chapman's single-seater racers, while Lunn – ever mindful of the way things were done in Detroit – demanded a hefty steel structure. Largely as a result, Broadley eased himself out to go his own way with the instantly successful Lola T70 sports racer, leaving Lunn to wrestle with a heavyweight flop called the Ford GT40 because it was only 40 inches (1016mm) high. But it looked sensational and the publicity men back in Detroit hailed it as a world-beater before it had spun a wheel. This made the shock even greater when all three GT40s failed to finish at Le Mans in 1964, soundly beaten by Ferraris.

Ford blamed the disaster, not on meddling where they had no knowledge, but on having failed to exercise sufficient control over a project beyond their shores. So they brought it back home for Lunn to begin work on a Mark II variant in Detroit, as the British factory concentrated on turning the original into a road car so that it could be homologated for GT racing. Power was simultaneously stepped up with a Cobra 289 cu in (4.7-litre) engine replacing the earlier 4.2-litre unit. Ford's humiliation was complete when they were beaten by a General Motors'-financed special called the Chaparral at Sebring in 1965.

The Mark II was then given a souped-up 427 cu

inch engine (7 litres) from the Galaxie sedan. The weight was awesome, but so was the power, no less than 427bhp with a monumental amount of torque. Ford's new computers had worked out that the revised bodyshape offered minimal wind resistance. These cars were blindingly fast but reduced their drivers to quivering wrecks as they tried to take off in testing at Le Mans. Nobody in Detroit had thought of programming their computers to calculate aerodynamic lift. Last minute additions of Ferrari-style spoilers enabled the Mark IIs to roar ahead of the opposition before burning out their transmissions. Four GT40s also cracked up, along with the works Ferraris, but old Enzo had the last laugh as victory fell to a private Ferrari 250LM – in effect a mid-engined 250GTO – running in the prototype class because of failure to homologate it as a GT car.

Although enraged by their failure at Le Mans, the Americans were learning fast and redesigned the Mark II into a far lighter and more sophisticated J-car. Unfortunately not all the lessons had been learned and it still had a homely two-speed automatic transmission and did not run well in testing. So eight 7-litre Mark IIs and five 4.7-litre GT40s lined up with three front-line Ferraris at Le Mans in 1966. Three Mark IIs survived the hard-fought contest for Henry Ford to flag them in 1-2-3 on 'the best day of his life.'

Meanwhile, enough GT40s had been produced for the model to be homologated for GT racing as Ferrari fought back to humble Ford by taking first three places on Ford's home ground at Daytona early in 1967. Ford responded by making the J-car a racing reality as the Mark IV with cleaned-up bodywork. This became the first car to exceed 200mph (322km/h) on the Mulsanne straight at Le Mans, as one of 11 Fords survived to win again.

The regulations were then changed to outlaw such monsters and Wyer enlisted support from Gulf Oil in America to run a private team of improved GT40s called Mirages. These cars swept all before them to win, not just Le Mans, but the world endurance championship in 1968.

By now the chief opposition came from Porsche with sports racing cars of ever-increasing engine capacity, but the glorious old GT40s – in Mirage form – fought on to win at Le Mans again, with Belgian star Jacky Ickx hanging on to pip Hans Herrman's works 3-litre Porsche 908 by just 100 yards (91m) after 24 hours' racing.

At colossal expense, Porsche – like Ford before them – then built an unprecedented 25 of their fabulously fast 4.5-litre 917 sports racing prototypes to homologate the model to run at Le Mans and took over the Wyer team as well.

It was then that the Ford GT40's competition career came to an end; success had come to it fairly late in life when it was run by a fully experienced professional team. But the cars – of which around 120 were produced – live on as the last of the great racing cars which could be driven in any conditions on the road.

SPECIFICATION

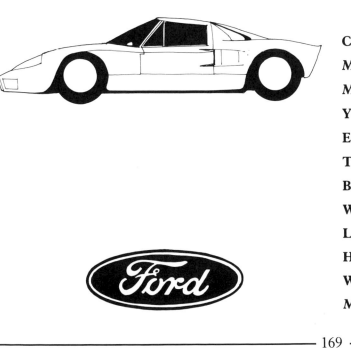

Country of origin: Great Britain.

Manufacturer: Ford.

Model: GT40.

Year: 1968.

Engine: V8 cylinder, overhead valve, 4736cc.

Transmission: 5 forward ratios, transaxle.

Body: Fixed-head coupé, 2 seats.

Wheelbase: 95in (2413mm).

Length: 169in (4293mm).

Height: 41in (1041mm).

Width: 70in (1778mm).

Maximum speed: 184mph (296km/h).

Ford V8 engine, 289 cu. in.,
271 bhp, mid-mounted.
Acceleration 0-60mph (0-96km/h)
in 5.9 secs. 0-100mph
(0-160 km/h) in
13.7 secs

Magnesium alloy wheels were
made by the racing cycle
accessory firm Campagnolo

DE TOMASO MANGUSTA

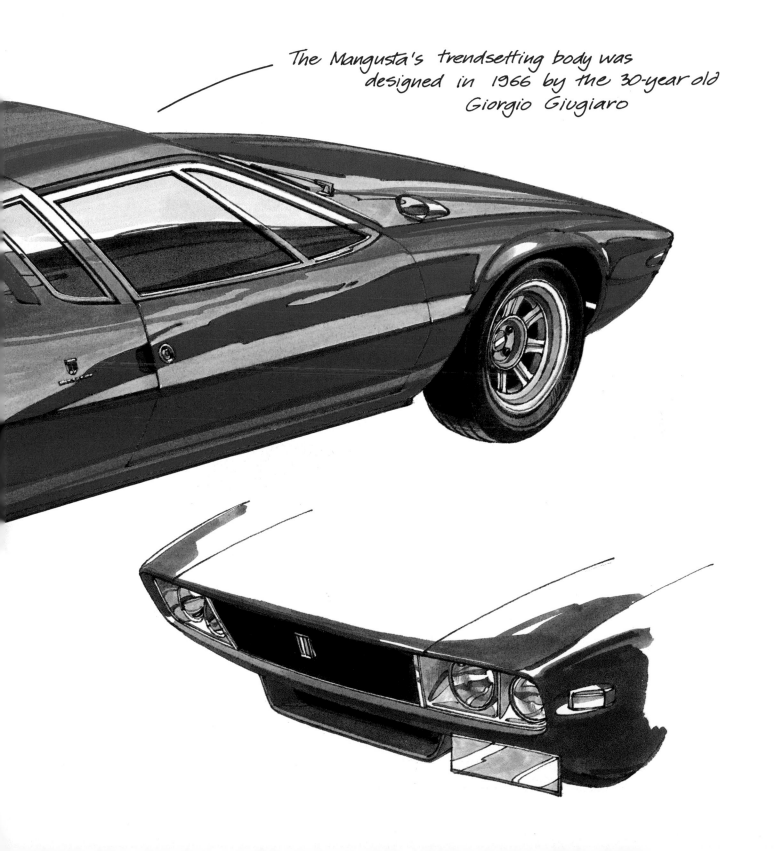

The Mangusta's trendsetting body was designed in 1966 by the 30-year old Giorgio Giugiaro

DE TOMASO MANGUSTA

THE MOTORING WORLD has seen few entrepreneurs more brilliant than the Argentinian racing driver Alejandro De Tomaso, who took up residence in Italy after daring to disagree with dictator Juan Peron, while his fellow student Ernesto 'Che' Guevara headed for Cuba. From his earliest days, the slight, dark-haired De Tomaso presented himself as a romantic rebel, and eventually married the tall blonde American Elizabeth Haskell, who was far more interested in changing the oil of her racing car than socialising with other wealthy young ladies. For a year or so, De Tomaso shared the driving seat of his sports-racing OSCA, made by the Maserati brothers, with his wife, who adopted the Spanish version of her name, Isabel. Then they set up as manufacturers in a shed in the shadow of the Ferrari works at Modena, Northern Italy. Ever one to cock a snoot at authority, De Tomaso promptly started making cars aimed at capturing established markets, notably that of Maserati's rival, Ferrari.

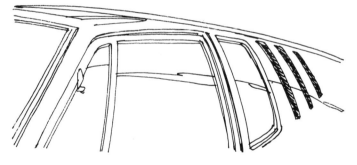

As Isabel laboured to instil some order into the creative chaos which reigned at De Tomaso Automobili, Alejandro dreamed up ever more exotic cars, drawing on the talents of numerous specialists who had established themselves around the Ferrari factory, to turn his ideas into reality. The one thing these cars lacked was development, because De Tomaso always dreamed of selling the design to a major manufacturer, and so generating finance for further projects that he could produce himself. By 1965 he had a small sports car, named the Vallelunga after the race track near Rome, heading for small-scale production with a Ford Cortina engine and backbone chassis like the Lotus Elan.

And then a new idea gelled in his fertile brain: why not turn it into his own version of a Ford GT40? All he would need to do was scale up the chassis, fit a Cobra engine and transmission, and hire somebody to design a stunning new body. The engines would be no problem. Carroll Shelby, who was running the Cobras in GT racing, was an old friend and could arrange supplies. De Tomaso could not help noticing, however, that despite Ford's advanced new iron casting technology, the engine was still very heavy and that Colin Chapman of Lotus was winning at Indianapolis with alloy-blocked experimental versions. There was not much hope of persuading Ford to part with those engines so De Tomaso did a deal with Chapman and between them they financed their own alloy castings. De Tomaso proclaimed the result as his brilliant new 500bhp engine, although it contained no pistons, crankshaft or connecting rods. As ever, he hoped somebody would come along and pay to put it into production.

Meanwhile, the Italian coachbuilders Ghia – who were producing Vallelunga bodies among others – had fallen upon hard times, with their effective owner, Rafael Trujillo, son of the former Dominican dictator, languishing in jail. With the help of Isabel's family, who ran the giant American electronics firm Rowan Controllers, De Tomaso took over Ghia so that the firm now had its own organisation for designing prototypes. One of the first appointments was that of the brilliant young designer, Giorgio Giugiaro who was eager for a new showcase for his work, after the relative anonymity of the old-established Bertone empire. As Giugiaro set to work on the new project – and numerous others – De Tomaso came up with an inspired name: Mangusta, which is Italian for mongoose, the small creature which eats Cobras for breakfast!

Many aspects of the Mangusta's design were

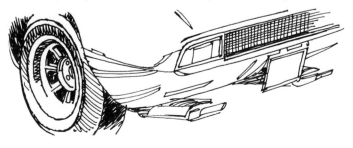

brilliant, others far from practical. The centre of gravity, for instance, was reduced by lowering the bulky power train so far that its output shaft passed under the final drive rather than above it in a conventional manner. The lack of ground clearance that resulted would have been quite acceptable on the track, but led to considerable problems on the road, as did the enforced restrictions on the diameter of the clutch, which meant that a very heavy triple-plate racing unit had to be used: all very well for lithe young racing drivers, but not so good for well-heeled poseurs! As ever, the new De Tomaso needed development.

But the body was something else, representing Giugiaro at his best. Its purity of line highlighted the mechanical parts which gave the car its power. Among the most obvious aspects of a contemporary racing machine were the awe-inspiring air intakes of vertical Weber carburettors. Normally it would be impossible to expose these trumpets in a road-going application because of problems associated with dust and debris. As everybody else reluctantly kept them under cover, Giugiaro gave the Mangusta a gullwing bonnet with windows showing off the machinery, set at such an angle that they provided rearward vision too. Thus, when interested spectators gazed down at a Mangusta at rest, they saw those wonderful carburettor trumpets, and when the owner drove off, he heard the engine's bellow and saw them in his rear view mirror. Then when he raised the bonnet to show off more of his wonderful machinery, the Mangusta looked just like some prehistoric bird of prey.

Of such cars legends are made, and this was certainly the case with the Mangusta, which threatened to swallow its occupants as the chassis flexed and gave it understeer and oversteer all in one fell swoop. But it looked fantastic and could not fail to catch the eye of Henry Ford. Scorned by Ferrari, his company was still suffering from a massive inferiority complex when the Mangusta appeared in 1966. He remembered how the first Henry Ford had failed to buy Isotta Fraschini in 1930, and since he had an Italian-born wife, Cristina, he was determined to buy his own Italian car company to show that Americans did have good taste, and to create new showroom traffic at the same time. After Fiat had beaten him to it and acquired Lancia, he swooped on the American-owned De Tomaso, much to Alejandro's delight.

The Mangusta gave Ford problems enough, as did the Pantera which followed, despite a conventional bodyshell to replace the flexing backbone chassis. Ford eventually sold everything except Ghia, which has been retained as a European styling studio of exceptional quality. De Tomaso then took back his more fully developed Pantera, and with Italian government aid and with Isabel by his side, built an empire which included his first love, Maserati.

SPECIFICATION

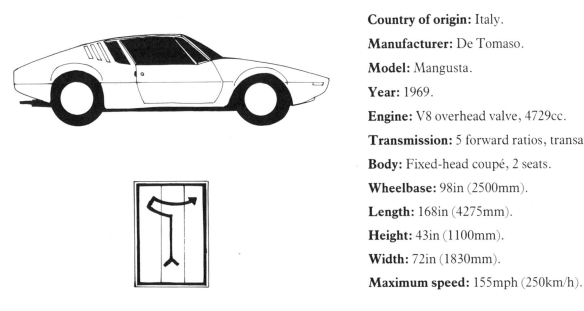

Country of origin: Italy.

Manufacturer: De Tomaso.

Model: Mangusta.

Year: 1969.

Engine: V8 overhead valve, 4729cc.

Transmission: 5 forward ratios, transaxle.

Body: Fixed-head coupé, 2 seats.

Wheelbase: 98in (2500mm).

Length: 168in (4275mm).

Height: 43in (1100mm).

Width: 72in (1830mm).

Maximum speed: 155mph (250km/h).

Prototype body was designed and built by Pininfarina in Turin, but production cars were manufactured by Scaglietti in Modena. The body shell was steel with aluminium doors, boot lid and bonnet

Classic early nose styling, with fixed headlamps under plastic covers

US export models featured 'pop-up' headlights to conform with American legislation

FERRARI DAYTONA

Campagnolo wheels

This car was called the Daytona by everybody except Enzo Ferrari who called it the 365 GTB/4

THE 365GTB/4, CALLED the Daytona by almost everybody except Enzo Ferrari, has been hailed as one of his greatest masterpieces because it was the last of a classic line of front-engined grand touring cars. As such, it occupies a position equal to that of his last great front-engined racing car, the 250GTO.

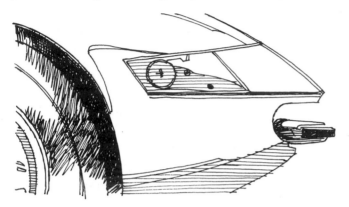

The 365 part of Ferrari's designation denoted the capacity in cubic centimetres of one of the cylinders of Colombo's V12 which reached its climax in this model. Ferrari was anxious that his grand touring cars should not suffer with the advent of new American exhaust emission regulations in 1968, so he had the overall size increased to 4.4 litres, to give 352bhp and a performance which showed that they were far more honest horses than the pony cars claimed! The top speed alone of 174mph (280km/h) ensured that the 365GTB/4 would become a legend.

The final figure 4, of course, stood for the four overhead camshafts with which this engine had been endowed in the earlier 4-litre touring car form developed from the more highly tuned single overhead cam units used in cars like the 250GTO and Testa Rossa. The initials GT were obvious, with the B showing that this was a *berlinetta,* or small saloon, rather than an S for spider, or open carriage with a minimum of bodywork: a style originally developed for horse-racing.

Ferrari's refusal to be ruffled by the success of the contemporary mid-engined Lamborghini Miura might have been seen as reactionary, but the way in which the 365GTB/4 was laid out certainly was not. Its superbly crafted engine was set as far back in the chassis as possible and linked to a transaxle at the

back for the best balance, in distinct contrast to its rivals which had their engines and transmission in the front or behind the seats. There was nothing to better the handling or stability of these Ferraris in the days before tyre technology, developed on mid-engined racing cars, was adapted for the road.

The styling, which established trends others would follow for more than two decades, was the work of Pininfarina's brilliant 28 year-old designer Leonardo Fioravanti, who had already set the automotive world alight with his mid-engined Ferrari Dino 206GT. He was to say later: 'Not only were the proportions of the car good, but the engine was also the best. There were no noise level restrictions and that allowed the famous top speed. I liked that . . . I was very young, you understand!'

Suffice it to say that nothing since has conveyed his slingshot look as dramatically as the 365GTB/4 Ferrari. When viewed in terms of absolute formations, the lines followed the classical family format of the long low nose established on the 250GTO with the short tail and small cabin of previous berlinetta racing cars serving to concentrate the most muscular mass at the back, like a jungle cat about to spring.

Yet the 365GTB/4 was far from clumsy. Its sleek nose formed a horizontal sharp edge from which the planes of the upper and lower bodywork swept away in streamlined curves, the corners emphasised by bumpers as delicate as the swordblades that used to be made by Modenese metalworkers. The rear edge of the bonnet was scalloped up to follow the curve of the windscreen and provide easy exit for hot air from the engine compartment at the same time as it eliminated the one-time problem of where to park the windscreen wipers, elegantly out of sight, yet ready for instant action.

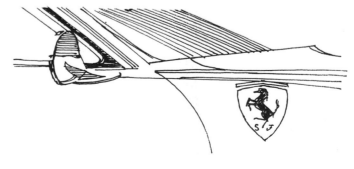

The aerodynamics were also improved to a startling degree by such attention to detail. The large, delicately curved, windscreen was attached to the body without a visible rubber seal, not only further improving the streamlining, but enhancing the new Ferrari's purity of line. A large flat rear window performed the same function allied to a larger expanse of glass than on similar GT cars. This provided better visibility with further harmony of line along the sides. The only feature which looked strange on initial inspection was the style of the dainty door handles, tiny latches almost concealed in the tops of the doorskins. Such a car demanded something more 'muscular', until one realised that if anything else had been used it would have cluttered the smooth flanks.

Some people immediately acclaimed this feat of styling as a masterpiece, others were not sure: they criticised the wide glass panel which covered the four headlights as being impractical; indeed, it had to be deleted for the American market which decreed against anything other than exposed lights and had forced Jaguar to change their E type at the same time. But most of the reaction against the 365GTB/4 stemmed from those who had expected it to be a scaled-up Dino, with a mid-engined configuration like the Miura. There were even people who complained that the five-spoke alloy wheels looked like those of a Porsche, but it was all sour grapes: these purposeful and elegant sculptures were exactly the same as those on contemporary formula one Ferraris, and there could be no higher praise.

Although the body was designed by Pininfarina, it was built by Scaglietti, who, for once, did not deviate from the original drawings. And with sales climbing safely after the coupé's introduction at the 1968 Paris Salon, a spider version was shown at Frankfurt the following year. With suitable out-of-sight reinforcements by Scaglietti, this open model was an immediate success with customers in warm climates like California, although the majority still ordered the fixed-head coupé because that was what was used (for better aerodynamics) in competition. Some owners even had their cars modified for races such as Le Mans and Daytona in which the big coupés were not disgraced by much lighter mid-engined opposition.

Then, ironically, wealthy enthusiasts started having the tops chopped off their cars to convert them into the spiders which now had a higher value because of their rarity, with the result that there were far more spiders on the road than ever left the Scaglietti works.

And why did Enzo Ferrari refuse to call the Daytona – so named by enthusiastic American customers after their national endurance racing track – by this name? Firstly, because he did not recognise it as a competition car, and, mainly, because the name was not his own idea!

SPECIFICATION

Country of origin: Italy.

Manufacturer: Ferrari.

Model: Daytona Spyder.

Year: 1969.

Engine: V12 cylinder, twin overhead camshaft, 4390cc.

Transmission: 5 forward ratios, transaxle.

Body: Fixed-head coupé, 2 seats.

Wheelbase: 94in (2400mm).

Length: 174in (4425mm).

Height: 49in (1245mm).

Width: 69in (1760mm).

Maximum speed: 174mph (280km/h).

Lightweight steel body panels
(and glassfibre where practical) reduced
body weight to 2000 lb (907 kg)
compared with the standard 911S

Carrera engine was bored
out to 2.8 litres for circuit
racing use

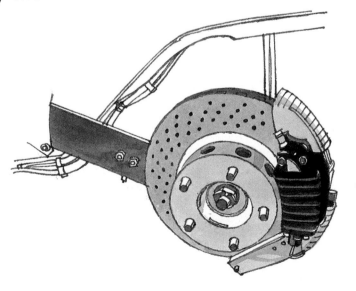

Ventilated disc brakes
on all four wheels

PORSCHE CARRERA RS

Special lightweight Glaverbel glass
was used as a further aid
to weight saving

Ever since Porsche gained their first major victory on the American continent, in Mexico's Carrera Panamericana road race of 1954, their best road cars have been called Carreras. And there has never been one greater than the RS (for *Rennsport* [literally racing sport]) built in 1972 and 1973. It remains the absolute classic of the seemingly timeless 911 series because it has the most responsive power-to-weight ratio, particularly in its lightest and most spartan form . . . and Porsche 911s are machines with the reflexes of predatory animals.

The Carrera RS was born of necessity at a time when Porsche were faced with technological development run riot in their fabulous 12-cylinder 917 racing cars. The costs of developing these endurance racing machines, with turbochargers providing as much as 1100bhp, were more than they could afford, especially as all opposition was fading away. This meant that rules would soon be changed to ensure closer racing, with the potential for all that research and expenditure going to waste. In any case, it was becoming more than apparent that such beasts bore little resemblance to anything which could be driven on the road and provided little profit in the sales to cost of development ratio.

So Porsche's chairman, Dr Ernst Fuhrmann – who had designed the first Carrera engine 20 years earlier – ordered the basic production car, the 911, to be prepared once more for racing. His sales department were against it to a man: such exercises meant that a large number of cars would have to be produced in a specification which was hard to sell to customers expecting more comfort than a competition driver. And the model could not be exported to the company's largest market, America, because of emission regulations. But Fuhrmann was adamant and he had the backing of the founder's son, Ferry Porsche, who was horrified at the costs of racing the 917.

Porsche had already failed to get the 911 homologated for saloon car racing because the back seats were far too small, so they concentrated on GT racing, in which Porsche customers were still competing with modified versions of the top-of-the-range 911S. The initial plan was to build 500 special versions of the 911S to homologate it for group 4 GT events, although going by the track record of the previous model, the 911R made until 1970, the price would have to be kept low to sell them in stripped-down competition form. Fuhrmann then 'encouraged' the sales department by decreeing that all Porsche executives eligible to drive a top model had to have a Carrera!

The 2.2-litre 911R – bored out to 2.3 litres as allowed under group 4 regulations – had performed best at minimal weight, so Carrera development followed the same lines. But now the capacity of the standard models had been increased to 2.4 litres to give them more torque for the American market, where constant gearchanging was unpopular, so there were lightweight 911s racing with 2.5-litre engines. The Carrera had to go one better so it was given a 2.7-litre engine which could be stretched to the maximum possible between the cylinder head studs for a 2.8-litre racing version built to exacting standards.

Meanwhile development engineer Norbert Singer pared no less than 200lb (90kg) off the weight of the already nimble 911S by using thinner steel body panels and glass fibre where they were not stressed.

Special lightweight Glaverbel glass was also used with the minimum of interior trim and no rear seats, a lot more weight being saved by the deletion of the 911's rubberised underside sealing. A final few pounds were shed by using an alloy front crossmember and Bilstein, rather than Koni, shock absorbers

The rest of the running gear was virtually standard apart from uprated anti-roll bars and suspension geometry marginally revised to incorporate new settings for wider rear wheels. A distinctive duck's tail spoiler was also moulded into the engine lid to achieve a dramatic reduction in rear-end lift and a consequent improvement in high-speed stability. This wheel/tyre/suspension and spoiler combination gave the Carrera RS the greatest cornering power of any production Porsche so far and the engine with the most power and torque.

The rear wings bulged out to cover the new rear wheels, which had the added advantage of allowing even wider rims to be fitted on pure racing examples contesting the more exotic group five class. This was because the regulations laid down that the width of cars homologated into group four could be increased by two inches (50mm) each side for the next class up. Because the Carrera RS was intended primarily as a competition car, it was available at first only with the strongest body, that of the fixed-head coupé.

Staff at the Porsche factory in Stuttgart were more surprised than anyone when the Carrera RS received such a rapturous reception on its introduction at the Paris Salon that all 500 were sold within a week! Production plans then had to be hurriedly revised so that more could be built. Demand from America was met by fitting the 911S engine, which gave only marginally less performance on lower gear ratios. Finally Porsche managed to squeeze in a further 1300 Carrera RS cars, many of which were fitted with the more luxurious 911S interior as a modification which would not affect homologation.

A happy side effect was that once the 1000 mark had been passed, the Carrera RS was then homologated into the group three category where opposition was far less formidable. Between 50 and 60 normal RS models were then taken off the production lines to be reworked as Carrera RSRs with full-race 2.8-litre engines for group five. But no matter which group they competed in, the Carreras were outstandingly successful as machines which were far closer to racing cars than any of their rivals.

The success story could not go on forever, though, as impending American safety regulations meant that the 911's bodyshell had to be modified with far heavier bumpers to survive in the vital American market, leaving the Carrera RS as the last of the really lightweight Porsche 911s. The cars which followed inevitably grew heavier, and were soon turbocharged to retain their performance, but they lost the lithe handling which made the RS the greatest of all.

SPECIFICATION

Country of origin: West Germany.

Manufacturer: Porsche.

Model: Carrera RS.

Year: 1972.

Engine: 6-cylinder horizontally-opposed, overhead camshaft, air cooled, 2687cc.

Transmission: 5 forward ratios, transaxle.

Body: Fixed-head coupé, 2 plus 2 seats.

Wheelbase: 89in (2261mm).

Length: 164in (4163mm).

Height: 52in (1321mm).

Width: 65in (1661mm).

Maximum speed: 150mph (241km/h).

CSL coupé developed
for American IMSA
racing featured heavily
swollen, ventilated
wheel arches

The 'L' in CSL stood for
lightweight in German, and
the car had light alloy doors and
bonnet with a steel boot lid to resist
the downforce created by its rear wing
points. The car shown here is the 3153cc model
capable of more than 140mph (225km/h)

The racing wing kit – 'Batwings' indeed!
Airflow aligning wing across top of rear
window and inverted aerofoil section on
the boot lid

BMW 3.0CSL BATMOBILE

BMW 3.0CSL BATMOBILE

THE SHOCK WAVES of Ford's pursuit of a high-performance image were still reverberating more than a decade after the original directive from Detroit, as the company's German arm chased glory in the European Touring Car championship. Nothing was more likely to cause trouble in the German motor industry, which had for years followed a policy summed up by Ferry Porsche when his designers suggested making a four-door Porsche: 'Shoemaker, stick to your last'.

In the eyes of the captains of the motor industry, Porsche made sports cars, Mercedes luxury saloon cars, BMW high-quality touring cars, Ford of Germany and Opel cheaper saloons and Volkswagen the 'Beetle', which was completely classless. Now Ford were preparing for a head-on clash with BMW by promoting their new Capri in saloon car racing.

The furore which followed saw innocent coupés turned into snarling prototype racers sprouting weird aerodynamic devices, the public showered with go-faster goodies in the sacred name of homologation, tyres reaching Formula One proportions, speeds rocketing and highly-paid grand prix stars taking over from regular racers in an attempt to tame the new monsters.

The European Touring Car championship had seen nothing like the day Ford stole a march on BMW with modified Capris. Before that, saloon car competition meant little more than tuning the engine mildly, driving down to a circuit, slapping on a set of racing wheels and flogging the car until the chequered flag fell. The Bayerische Motoren Werke were not unduly worried that their four-cylinder 2002 was slower than Alfa Romeo's GTAm. It was heavier, but more reliable, so it sometimes won. Sales were never threatened.

But Ford were hungry for success. So they took the extreme measure of producing 1000 lightweight Capris to homologate them as a special model for this sort of competition. It meant making all sorts of special parts, but eventually they won, leaving BMW aghast that anybody should dare to challenge Bavaria's prestige car.

Their 2800CS had looked so innocuous when it first appeared in the 1969 Spa 24-hour race. The big coupé still sported power steering and wallowed along on road suspension, consuming no less than 40 tyres before it crossed the line a perspiring ninth. But this was the car that had to put the Capris in their place, because the engine of the more agile 2002 was too small. BMW's need was pressing, so they hired Jochen Neerpasch and Martin Braungart, who had transformed the Capri, to develop the coupé.

When they arrived at BMW from Ford, the racing Capri was about three-quarters the weight of the big BMW with roughly the same 300bhp to propel both models. Almost immediately, BMW built a run of 1000 3.0CSL coupés with ultra-lightweight thin-gauge steel and alloy bodies to homologate a new model at a lower weight before listing it with the option of competition suspension, very wide quick-change centre-lock racing wheels, a five speed gearbox, pressure-cooled final drive, magnesium castings in place of iron, massive four-piston racing brakes, and a 3.3-litre dry sump engine producing 350bhp. These changes put the BMW on a par with the Ford Capri, But Neerpasch and Braungart knew they would not be enough to ensure victory.

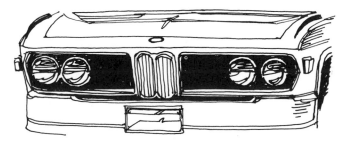

Then they spotted a new clause in the racing regulations which allowed 'evolutionary' changes to existing cars. The idea was to allow privateers with limited means to update older cars to a similar specification to the new models fielded by the factories. Otherwise there was a risk of the championship running short of competition for the top teams. Neerpasch and Braungart chose to interpret the spirit rather than the letter of the rules and realised they presented no obstacle to evolutionary changes to the factory's own latest cars!

With only days to go before the last homologation date for the new season in 1973, they developed a set of aerodynamic aids for the 3.0CSL, based on the wings they had seen on the Porsche 917 endurance racing cars. These new parts made the 3.0CSL much more stable at high speed and lopped no less than 15 seconds off their previous fastest lap of the tortuous Nurburgring racing circuit, thus beating the Capri's time by 10 seconds.

Ford were left trailing, not allowed to add even a tiny spoiler to their boot lids after the homologation deadline, when the winged 3.0CSL BMW appeared, bearing the nickname Batmobile after the TV comic strip hero's fabled flying car. The Batmobiles were still heavier than the Capris but soon had the advantage of 370bhp from 3.5-litre engines. It is ironic to note that the optional wings, splitters and air dams had to be packed in the boots of German-specification BMWs because strict environmental regulations did not allow the fitting of any 'sharp-looking' additions to the body!

Despite drastic cutbacks on expenditure in the wake of the winter's oil crisis, Ford managed to homologate a four overhead cam 445bhp variant of their engine in a winged Capri for the 1974 season. This took the car up to the weight of a Batmobile, which now had 450bhp from a 24-valve engine! The scene was set for a fitting climax to the heavyweight championship of the saloon car racing world, but the two contenders flagged through lack of cash and the contest faltered as sales of sporting cars plunged during the oil crisis.

Ford had to quit, and with only hollow victories in sight, BMW took their Batmobiles to America to promote sales through local IMSA racing. They returned to Europe in 1976 for a new silhouette endurance racing formula in which they challenged Porsche with a 750bhp Batmobile, the turbocharger of which generated so much heat that the floor glowed red.

In the European Touring Car championship they faced a new challenge at last from British Jaguars. Sadly, the ailing British Motor Corporation could not make up for the years of experience BMW had gained in such competitions and failed to provide any real opposition. Much the same applied in endurance racing, where Porsches left the heavier Batmobiles behind. BMW knew when they were beaten and retired happy in the knowledge that they had defended their reputation in saloon car racing. As ever, it was a case of 'Shoemaker, stick to your last!'

SPECIFICATION

Country of origin: West Germany.

Manufacturer: BMW.

Model: 3.0CSL Batmobile.

Year: 1973.

Engine: 6-cylinder in-line, overhead valve, 3153cc.

Transmission: 4 forward ratios.

Body: Fixed-head coupé, 4 seats.

Wheelbase: 103in (2620mm).

Length: 182in (4630mm).

Height: 54in (1370mm).

Width: 68in (1730mm).

Maximum speed: 137mph (220km/h).

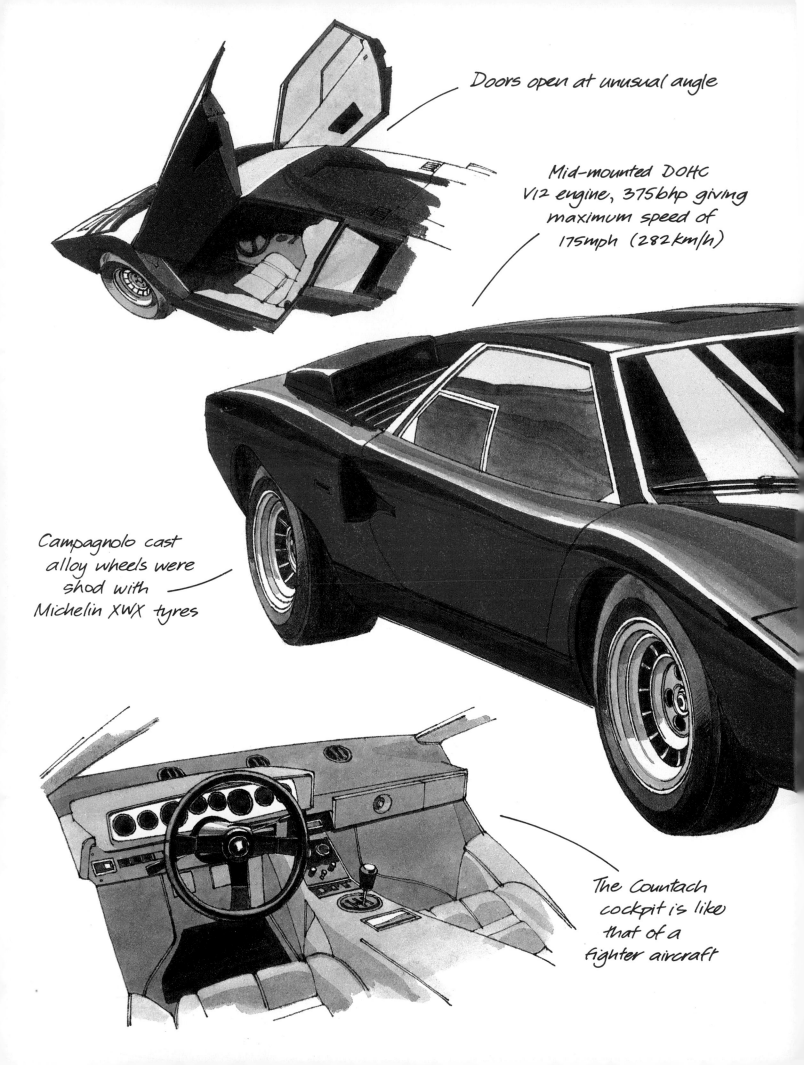

Doors open at unusual angle

Mid-mounted DOHC V12 engine, 375bhp giving maximum speed of 175mph (282km/h)

Campagnolo cast alloy wheels were shod with Michelin XWX tyres

The Countach cockpit is like that of a fighter aircraft

LAMBORGHINI COUNTACH

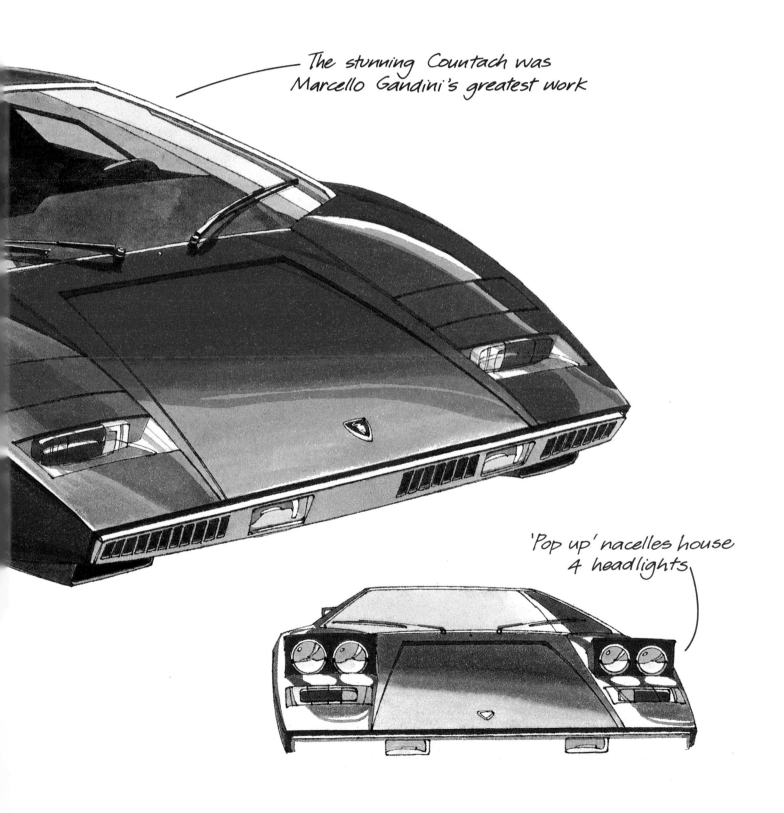

The stunning Countach was
Marcello Gandini's greatest work

'Pop up' nacelles house
4 headlights

NOBODY HAS BEEN able to make a car more exotic than the Lamborghini Countach since the first prototype was shown with a 5-litre engine in 1971: and it became a production reality with the famous 4-litre V12 in 1974. Every part of the Countach concept fits the description 'exotic' so perfectly: it is a strange car, stranger perhaps than almost any other, with lines that are fantastic, almost barbaric.

The Countach had an immaculately conceived forerunner in Lamborghini's first mid-engined car, the Miura, developed by three brilliant young engineers who hoped that Ferruccio Lamborghini would allow them to develop it into a racing car to beat the Ford GT40. But Ferruccio Lamborghini had more sense than to throw his money into the bottomless pit of racing with as close and vigorous a rival as Ferrari. He insisted with supreme logic that the Miura be kept as a road car to publicise his more profitable products, tractors and oil burners. 'Every Miura I build will be worth more than winning a grand prix. People will talk about it long after they have forgotten who won the last race,' he said with utter conviction.

One of the brilliant young men, Giampaulo Dallera, quit on the spot to pursue what he hoped would be a racing career with De Tomaso. But there were few jobs to equal the prestige of creating Lamborghinis, so the other two, Paulo Stanzani and New Zealander Bob Wallace, a former Maserati racing mechanic, stayed. Sparkling young minds need to be nourished, and Ferruccio Lamborghini did not object to Wallace burning the midnight oil to create a competition version of the Miura, called the Jota, just for fun.

Meanwhile, another bright young man, Marcello Gandini, who had made the Miura his first great work for Bertone, the bodybuilders, was designing a

car they called the Carabo, after the beetle it so resembled. The theme of this amazing showcar was continued in the futuristic Lancia Stratos of 1970. Slowly, but surely, the Countach was emerging from the chrysalis of its conception.

Stanzani, who was never afraid to take dramatic decisions, such as reversing the engine's direction of rotation, dispensed with the vagaries of the Miura's long floppy gear change by simply turning the engine through 90 degrees, so that it faced north to south, rather than east to west. Other people who had done this placed the clutch, gearbox and final drive at the back in the accepted order, but not Stanzani. He put the gearbox at the front, solving the long linkage problem with a stroke of the pen. The final drive remained behind the engine to balance the car better, with a shaft from the gearbox running through the sump. With the mass of the engine placed well forward, the Countach was less inclined to lift its nose than the tail-heavy Miura.

Eight years earlier, when Ferruccio Lamborghini had hired Giotto Bizzarrini from Ferrari to design his engine, he had shown great foresight in insisting that it be contained within a very low overall height for a V12. The idea then was to allow it to be fitted in the front of a car with a bonnet as low as that of a Jaguar E type. The result now was that the weight of the Countach was concentrated low, quite unlike that of its rival from Ferrari, the Berlinetta Boxer. Already the Countach was roaring ahead.

Gandini's bodywork was amazing, the ultimate expression of the wedge shape which for aerodynamic reasons had become popular on the race track, in that it promoted stability when cornering. The doors opened in a most striking fashion, like the wings of a beetle (or carabo). But most startling of all was the car's appearance, which prompted a name that was pure Bertone: Countach, a Piedmontese expression

of rude wonder and amazement. It was the first Lamborghini that Ferruccio had not named after a fighting bull.

It was also the last really exotic car he produced, the smaller Urraco remaining an unfinished masterpiece until repeated infusions of new blood and money put it into production in 1973. As Stanzani struggled to get the Urraco off the ground to meet Porsche and Ferrari head-on in the sports car arena, the sombre Stakhanovite Wallace worked almost alone to hone the Countach prototype to perfection. He was an uncompromising character and despite his experience with the Jota it took three years to produce the first car which could be sold to the fabulously wealthy.

When the definitive Countach supercar scythed away from the works at Sant'Agata in 1974 it had the well-tried 4-litre engine in place of the prototype's fragile 5-litre, and an incredible frame as complex and efficient as that of the Maserati Birdcage on which Wallace had worked 14 years earlier. Exotic aviation alloy and Belgian Glaverbel glass made the Countach lighter than the Miura which shared the same power. With a better balance and superior aerodynamics, the handling was in the realms of the fantastic. And so was the cost of building it. Lamborghini made almost everything themselves and when you realise that it took 17 men to cast one of their exquisite cylinder heads, you can imagine how high the labour costs were.

Lamborghini probably lost money on every Countach they made, such were the overheads of development in the marble palace at Sant'Agata. And they could not step up production to make the car more profitable because there was a limit to the number of men with the necessary skill to produce such machinery. As the years went by, Ferruccio Lamborghini sold his assets to stay alive and eventually retired to grow grapes. The occasional Countach still came out of Sant'Agata as ever-changing management struggled to maintain a legend. But even when Wallace and Stanzani followed Ferruccio away from the car which had become an obsession, others were willing to sacrifice themselves.

Then Dallera returned like a prodigal son to refine the Countach, which had become the symbol of everything brilliant in Italian industry. Pirelli designed new low-profile tyres to replace the deep traditional rubber, the flexing of which had caused Wallace so much heartache. A road car revolution was started by the stiff P7-clad Countach S of 1978. Still Automobili Lamborghini tottered from one financial crisis to another until stability was achieved by a French takeover in 1980 and the 5-litre engine at last developed into today's Quattrovalvole. But there is still nothing on the road which can match the speed, handling and style of a Countach: the classic among classics.

SPECIFICATION

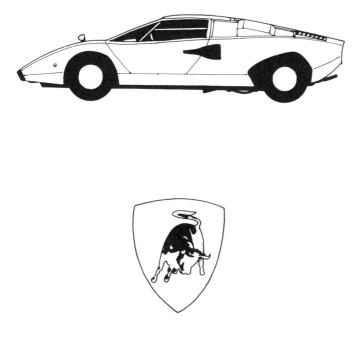

Country of origin: Italy.

Manufacturer: Lamborghini.

Model: Countach.

Year: 1974.

Engine: V12 cylinder, twin overhead camshaft, 3929cc.

Transmission: 5 forward ratios, frame-mounted final drive.

Body: Fixed-head coupé, 2 seats.

Wheelbase: 96in (2443mm).

Length: 163in (4140mm).

Height: 41in (1029mm).

Width: 74in (1890mm).

Maximum speed: 175mph (282km/h)

INDEX

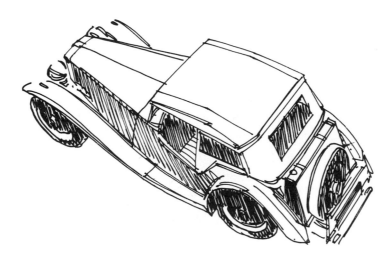